Y0-CPE-914

Geoffrey Chaucer

Merchant's Tale

Edited by
Robert J. Blanch
Northeastern University

The Merrill Literary Casebook Series
Edward P. J. Corbett, Editor

Charles E. Merrill Publishing Company
A Bell & Howell Company
Columbus, Ohio

For Ruth Fisher Smith

Copyright © 1970 by CHARLES E. MERRILL PUBLISHING
COMPANY, Columbus, Ohio. All rights reserved. No part
of this book may be reproduced in any form, electronic
or mechanical, including photocopy, recording, or any
information storage and retrieval system without permission in writing from the publisher.

Standard Book Number: 675-09346-5

Library of Congress Catalog Number: 79-110655

1 2 3 4 5 6 7 8 9 10 — 73 72 71 70

Printed in the United States of America

Foreword

The Charles E. Merrill Literary Casebook Series deals with short literary works, arbitrarily defined here as "works which can be easily read in a single sitting." Accordingly, the series will concentrate on poems, short stories, brief dramas, and literary essays. These casebooks are designed to be used in literature courses or in practical criticism courses where the instructor wants to expose his students to an extensive and intensive study of a single, short work or in composition courses where the instructor wants to expose his students to the discipline of writing a research paper on a literary text.

All of the casebooks in the series follow this format: (1) foreword; (2) general instructions for the writing of a research paper; (3) the editor's Introduction; (4) the text of the literary work; (5) a number of critical articles on the literary work; (6) suggested topics for short papers on the literary work; (7) suggested topics for long (10-15 pages) papers on the literary work; (8) a selective bibliography of additional readings on the literary work. Some of the casebooks, especially those dealing with poetry, may carry an additional section, which contains such features as variant versions of the work, a closely related literary work, comments by the author and his contemporaries on the work.

So that students might simulate first-hand research in library copies of books and bound periodicals, each of the critical articles carries full bibliographical information at the bottom of the first page of the article, and the text of the article carries the actual page-numbers of the original source. A notation like /131/ after a word in the text indicates that *after* that word in the original source the article went over to page 131. All of the text between that number and the next number, /132/, can be taken as occurring on page 131 of the original source.

Edward P.J. Corbett
General Editor

Contents

Introduction   1

Merchant's Tale by Geoffrey Chaucer   7

Notes   37

J. S. P. Tatlock, *Chaucer's* Merchant's Tale   43

G. G. Sedgewick, *The Structure of* The Merchant's Tale   57

Bertrand H. Bronson, *Afterthoughts on the Merchant's Tale*   68

Robert M. Jordan, *The Non-Dramatic Disunity of the* Merchant's Tale   81

Mortimer J. Donovan, *The Image of Pluto and Proserpine in the* Merchant's Tale   94

Paul A. Olson, *Chaucer's Merchant and January's* "Hevene in Erthe Heere"   105

Gertrude M. White, *"Hoolynesse or Dotage"*: *The Merchant's January*   116

Margaret Schlauch, *Chaucer's* Merchant's Tale *and Courtly Love*   124

J. A. Burrow, *Irony in the Merchant's Tale*   135

Robert J. Blanch, *Irony in Chaucer's* Merchant's Tale   144

Suggestions for Papers   150

Additional Readings   152

General Instructions For a Research Paper   155

Introduction

Since the modern reader is separated from Chaucer by six centuries and by radical changes in intellectual outlook, it is necessary to trace the background of some of the medieval conventions shared by Chaucer and his contemporaries. A clear knowledge of two of these medieval conventions—the penchant for symbolism and the cult of courtly love—may help the reader to gain a fuller understanding of the intellectual climate of the Middle Ages.

It is usually agreed that medieval man sought to invest spiritual mysteries with perceptible forms, to illuminate the dark secrets of God by piercing the veil of the supernatural. A favorite means of expressing the spiritual concretely was through the symbol, some material object signifying an abstract idea. Furthermore, medieval man found transcendental meaning in all created objects because he believed that earthly phenomena were valuable only insofar as they were signs of suprasensible realities emanating from God. Earthly phenomena, as Johan Huizinga reminds us, derived their ultimate meaning and *raison d'être* from God:

> Of no great truth was the medieval mind more conscious than of St. Paul's phrase: *Videmus nunc per speculum in aenigmate, tunc autem facie ad faciem.* The Middle Ages never forgot that all things would be absurd, if their meaning were exhausted in their function and their place in the phenomenal world, if by their essence they did not reach into a world beyond this.[1]

Stemming from this medieval conviction of transcendental meaning in all created objects is the view of the world as a book bearing the imprint of God, a book wherein every creature points to the wisdom of God.[2] By employing the medieval premise, ". . . through visible things we are moved toward the invisible,"[3] it may be possible to arrive at an understanding of the symbolic *Weltanschauung* of the Middle Ages.

---

[1] Johan Huizinga, *The Waning of the Middle Ages* (Garden City, N.Y., 1954), p. 201.
[2] Hugh of St. Victor, *Eruditionis didascalicae* (Migne, *Patrologia Latina*, CLXXVI, 814).
[3] Gulielmus Durandus, *Rationale divinorum officiorum* (Lugduni, 1559), I, iii, sec. 38.

1

All creatures of the sensible world lead the mind of the one aspiring after wisdom to the immutable God, for these creatures are, as St. Bonaventura says, "shadows, echoes, and pictures, the traces, simulacra, and reflections of that First Principle most powerful, wisest, and best. . . ."[4] True knowledge, then, consists not in scrutinizing the outward forms of material objects, but in penetrating to the inner kernel of truth revealed by God for human instruction. As elements of God's revelation, natural phenomena mirror, albeit imperfectly, Christ's redeeming sacrifice, the sacraments, and the eternal life of the blessed in Heaven.

Even the earthly cycle of seasons is linked symbolically with profound religious mysteries. Spring, for example, suggests the restoration of spiritual life through baptism, the resurrection of the body at the Last Judgment, and the beginning of good works.[5] Winter, on the other hand, adumbrates the tribulation and death imminent for mankind and the universe.[6]

With the establishment of a symbolic underpinning for the medieval view of the cosmos, the symbolic mode of thought permeated all phases of medieval life:

> The habit of the Mediaeval mind of reading into every leaf, and animal, and bird, and inanimate object, and number, and ecclesiastical vestment a mystical meaning, and using it to point out some moral, either true or fanciful, is one of the characteristics of that age.[7]

This symbolic habit was manifested in the architectonics of the Gothic cathedrals; in the statues and paintings of Christ, the saints and Old Testament patriarchs; and in the effulgent stained-glass windows, symbolic of the Divine Light. Medieval man also knew the symbolic character of alchemy and astrology; the mystical properties of the precious gems and metals, derived from St. John's *Apocalypse*; and the rich liturgy of the Mass.

To the medieval mind the Old Testament was, simultaneously, a prefiguration of the New Testament and a shadowy glimpse of the perfection of the cosmos. Even the love between man and woman was frequently linked with divine love, thereby becoming a "type" of the mystical bond between the soul and Christ, the Heavenly Bridegroom. In such a symbolic ethos, medieval literature flourished, culminating late in the fourteenth century in the unique genius of Geoffrey Chaucer's poetry.

---

[4] Saint Bonaventura, *The Mind's Road to God*, trans. George Boas (New York, 1953), p. 20.

[5] Rabanus Maurus, *De Universo* (Migne, *PL*, CXI, 302).

[6] Maurus, col. 303.

[7] F. R. Webber, *Church Symbolism* (Cleveland, 1938), p. 17.

Another medieval convention requiring explanation is the cult of courtly love. This unremitting concern with love started in Provence, with the poetry of the troubadours, at the end of the eleventh century. Although the key to the *ultimate* origin of courtly love cannot be found, the fundamental tenets of courtly love are clearly discerned. Essential to the concept of courtly love were the qualities of courtesy and humility. Dependent on distinctions of rank, courtesy in the Middle Ages designated, as John Gardner puts it, "the proper (not merely necessary) relationship of men to their superiors, their equals, and their inferiors on the social scale."[8] In terms of the courtly love relationship, the woman of the manor or court was superior in civilizing force and *politesse* to all males except her husband (if she were married). Since the man in *amour courtois* was inferior to his beloved lady, the service of love assumed a feudal context: the woman was the overlord; the man, a vassal. The male lover, always abject before his beloved lady, obeyed her slightest command joyfully and unquestioningly.

The inevitable outgrowth of this ideal of service was intense suffering for the male lover. Since the lover was frequently the victim of unrequited love, his burning desires for the lady increased, precipitated especially by visual stimuli. The goal kept retreating, however, and the male's desires often remained unsatiated. Perhaps the best expression of the suffering arising from courtly love may be found in Andreas Capellanus's *De arte honeste amandi*, a twelfth-century work which codified, whether half-humorously or not, the principles of courtly love:

> Love is a certain inborn suffering derived from the sight of and excessive meditation upon the beauty of the opposite sex, which causes each one to wish above all things the embraces of the other and by common desire to carry out all of love's precepts in the other's embrace.[9]

Whatever type of suffering courtly love effected, however, the seed of virtue was planted in man's passionate longing for his beloved. The intense desire and suffering became an abluent which cleansed the lover's character of its imperfections and offered him, through the beloved lady, a transcendent experience. In knightly combat, especially, was love an ennobling force, for the power of love increased the strength and boldness of the knight in armed conflict. The courtly lover, however, did not usually perform deeds of valor for any altruistic reason, but primarily to win the lady. He would embark on a series of physical adventures or

---

[8] John Gardner, ed. and trans., *The Complete Works of the Gawain-Poet* (Chicago, 1965), p. 53.

[9] Andreas Capellanus, *The Art of Courtly Love*, trans. J. J. Parry (New York, 1957), p. 2.

would fight any battle in order to capture his beloved's attention and to please her.

Since the lady in the medieval lyrics and romances could not be courted openly, frequently because she was already married, the lover was required to observe absolute secrecy. The secrecy of the courtly lover, as Peter Dronke points out, was not necessarily a façade for the concealment of adultery:

> There is the fear and anguish of love frustrated, by the woman's fear of losing her good name, by circumstances, by the outside world. . . . But this is not because love is always illicit. . . . The secrecy of *amour courtois* springs rather from the universal notion of love as a mystery not to be profaned by the outside world, not to be shared by any but lover and beloved.[10]

While adultery was not a distinguishing mark of courtly love, courtly love poets frequently used love-language derived from the theological and mystical traditions. The lady in the courtly love relationship was often described as a mediator between man and God, an angel, or a divine figure. This use of Christian imagery in *amour courtois* may represent a reaction against social and religious views on marriage and love.

In the Middle Ages, marriage was construed as a contractual arrangement, precipitated by social and financial considerations. Since parents were interested in uniting family estates through the marriage of their children, a bond of love between prospective marriage partners, although a remote possibility, was not a *desideratum*. Society's myopic outlook on marriage, moreover, was reinforced by traditional Church beliefs. To the medieval theologian the primary purposes of marriage were the procreation of children and the payment of the marriage debt. If these objectives were subordinate in value to passionate desire, then desire was a sin.

Plagued by the disparity between amatory and socio-religious ideals, the courtly-love poets created an erotic religion, a rival or parody of Christianity. Through this erotic religion the poets were enabled to step out of real life into a play world of wish-fulfillment. If passionate desire were considered to be unimportant, or even sinful, in the relations between the sexes, then the poets of *amour courtois* would mold love into a transcendent experience, an experience which bestows life and worth upon every human being. If medieval Christianity exhorted each individual to use his earthly life as a preparation for the eternal bliss of

---

[10] Peter Dronke, *Medieval Latin and the Rise of European Love-Lyric* (Oxford, 1965), I, 48.

heaven, then the courtly-love poets would identify the passionate relationship between a man and a woman on earth with the perfect happiness of the heavenly state. That human love be heaven itself was
obviously antithetical to the teachings of medieval Christianity. The play
world of *amour courtois,* however, was the only possible instrument
through which the medieval love poets could lash out against the beliefs
of their age, an age in which love was seldom necessary in marriage and
the natural passions of human beings were denied.

Merchant's Tale*

The Merchant's Prologue

"Wepyng and waylyng, care and oother sorwe
I knowe ynogh, on even and a-morwe,"   1214
Quod the Marchant, "and so doon other mo
That wedded been. I trowe that it be so,
For wel I woot it fareth so with me.
I have a wyf, the worste that may be,
For thogh the feend to hire ycoupled were,
She wolde hym overmacche, I dar wel swere.
What sholde I yow reherce in special   1221
Hir hye malice? She is a shrewe at al.
Ther is a long and large difference
Bitwix Grisildis grete pacience
And of my wyf the passyng crueltee.   1225
Were I unbounden, also moot I thee!
I wolde nevere eft comen in the snare.
We wedded men lyven in sorwe and care.
Assaye whoso wole, and he shal fynde
That I seye sooth, by Seint Thomas of Inde,
As for the moore part, I sey nat alle.   1231
God shilde that it sholde so bifalle!
    A! goode sire Hoost, I have ywedded bee
Thise monthes two, and moore nat, pardee,
And yet, I trowe, he that al his lyve   1235
Wyflees hath been, though that men wolde him ryve
Unto the herte, ne koude in no manere
Tellen so muchel sorwe as I now heere
Koude tellen of my wyves cursednesse!"
    "Now," quod oure Hoost, "Marchaunt, so God yow blesse,   1240

---

* The text of the *Merchant's Tale* printed here is based upon that found in *The Works of Geoffrey Chaucer*, ed. F. N. Robinson, Second Edition. Boston: Houghton Mifflin Company, 1957, with some minor alterations in spelling and punctuation.

Syn ye so muchel knowen of that art
Ful hertely I pray yow telle us part."
  "Gladly," quod he, "but of myn owene soore
For sory herte, I telle may namoore."

Merchant's Tale

  Whilom ther was dwellynge in Lumbardye
A worthy knyght that born was of Pavye,   1246
In which he lyved in greet prosperitee;
And sixty yeer a wyflees man was hee,
And folwed ay his bodily delyt
On wommen, ther as was his appetyt,   1250
As doon thise fooles that been seculeer.
And whan that he was passed sixty yeer,
Were it for hoolynesse or for dotage
I kan nat seye, but swich a greet corage   1254
Hadde this knyght to been a wedded man
That day and nyght he dooth al that he kan
T'espien where he myghte wedded be,
Preyinge oure Lord to graunten him that he
Mighte ones knowe of thilke blisful lyf
That is bitwixe an housbonde and his wyf,
And for to lyve under that hooly boond   1261
With which that first God man and womman bond.
"Noon oother lyf," seyde he, "is worth a bene,
For wedlok is so esy and so clene
That in this world it is a paradys."   1265
Thus seyde this olde knyght that was so wys.
  And certeinly, as sooth as God is kyng,
To take a wyf it is a glorious thyng,
And namely whan a man is oold and hoor;
Thanne is a wyf the fruyt of his tresor.   1270
Thanne sholde he take a yong wyf and a feir,
On which he myghte engendren hym an heir,
And lede his lyf in joye and in solas,
Where as thise bacheleris synge "allas,"
Whan that they fynden any adversitee   1275
In love, which nys but childyssh vanytee.
And trewely it sit wel to be so,
That bacheleris have often peyne and wo;

On brotel ground they buylde, and brotelnesse
They fynde whan they wene sikernesse. 1280
They lyve but as a bryd or as a beest
In libertee, and under noon arreest.
Ther as a wedded man in his estaat
Lyveth a lyf blisful and ordinaat,
Under this yok of mariage ybounde. 1285
Wel may his herte in joy and blisse habounde,
For who kan be so buxom as a wyf?
Who is so trewe and eek so ententyf
To kepe hym, syk and hool, as is his make?
For wele or wo she wole hym nat forsake; 1290
She nys nat wery hym to love and serve,
Thogh that he lye bedrede til he sterve.
And yet somme clerkes seyn it nys nat so,
Of whiche he Theofraste is oon of tho.
What force though Theofraste liste lye? 1295
"Ne take no wyf," quod he, "for housbondrye,
As for to spare in houshold thy dispence.
A trewe servant dooth moore diligence
Thy good to kepe than thyn owene wyf,
For she wol clayme half part al hir lyf. 1300
And if that thou be syk, so God me save,
Thy verray freendes or a trewe knave
Wol kepe thee bet than she that waiteth ay
After thy good and hath doon many a day.
And if thou take a wyf unto thyn hoold, 1305
Ful lightly maystow been a cokewold."
This sentence and an hundred thynges worse
Writeth this man, ther God his bones corse!
But take no kep of al swich vanytee;
Deffie Theofraste, and herke me. 1310
    A wyf is Goddes yifte verraily;
Alle othere manere yiftes hardily,
As londes, rentes, pasture, or commune,
Or moebles, alle been yiftes of Fortune,
That passen as a shadwe upon a wal. 1315
But drede nat, if pleynly speke I shal,
A wyf wol laste and in thyn hous endure
Wel lenger than thee list, paraventure.
    Mariage is a ful greet sacrement.
He which that hath no wyf, I holde hym shent;
He lyveth helplees and al desolat,— 1321
I speke of folk in seculer estaat.

And herke why I sey nat this for noght
That womman is for mannes helpe ywroght.
The hye God, whan he hadde Adam maked
And saugh him al allone, bely-naked,   1326
God of his grete goodnesse seyde than,
"Lat us now make an helpe unto this man
Lyk to hymself"; and thanne he made him Eve.
Heere may ye se, and heerby may ye preve
That wyf is mannes helpe and his confort,   1331
His paradys terrestre, and his disport.
So buxom and so vertuous is she,
They moste nedes lyve in unitee.   1334
O flessh they been, and o fleesh, as I gesse,
Hath but oon herte in wele and in distresse.
    A wyf! a, Seinte Marie, *benedicite!*
How myghte a man han any adversitee
That hath a wyf? Certes, I kan nat seye.
The blisse which that is bitwixe hem tweye
Ther may no tonge telle or herte thynke.   1341
If he be povre, she helpeth hym to swynke;
She kepeth his good and wasteth never a deel;
Al that hire housbonde lust hire liketh weel;
She seith nat ones "nay," whan he seith "ye."   1345
"Do this," seith he; "Al redy, sire," seith she.
O blisful ordre of wedlok precious,
Thou art so murye and eek so vertuous,
And so commended and appreved eek
That every man that halt hym worth a leek,
Upon his bare knees oughte al his lyf   1351
Thanken his God that hym hath sent a wyf,
Or elles preye to God hym for to sende
A wyf to laste unto his lyves ende.
For thanne his lyf is set in sikernesse;   1355
He may nat be deceyved, as I gesse,
So that he werke after his wyves reed.
Thanne may he boldely beren up his heed,
They been so trewe and therwithal so wyse;
For which, if thou wolt werken as the wyse,
Do alwey so as wommen wol thee rede.   1361
    Lo, how that Jacob, as thise clerkes rede,
By good conseil of his mooder Rebekke,
Boond the kydes skyn aboute his nekke,
For which his fadres benyson he wan.   1365
    Lo Judith, as the storie eek telle kan,

By wys conseil she Goddes peple kepte,
And slow hym Olofernus whil he slepte.
   Lo Abigayl, by good conseil, how she
Saved hir housbonde Nabal whan that he   1370
Sholde han be slayn; and looke, Ester also
By good conseil delyvered out of wo
The peple of God, and made hym Mardochee
Of Assuere enhaunced for to be.
   Ther nys no thyng in gree superlatyf,   1375
As seith Senek, above an humble wyf.
   Suffre thy wyves tonge, as Catoun bit;
She shal comande, and thou shalt suffren it,
And yet she wole obeye of curteisye.
A wyf is kepere of thyn housbondrye;   1380
Wel may the sike man biwaille and wepe,
Ther as ther nys no wyf the hous to kepe.
I warne thee, if wisely thou wolt wirche,
Love wel thy wyf, as Crist loved his chirche.
If thou lovest thyself, thou lovest thy wyf;
No man hateth his flessh, but in his lyf   1386
He fostreth it, and therfore bidde I thee,
Cherisse thy wyf, or thou shalt nevere thee.
Housbonde and wyf, what so men jape or pleye,
Of worldly folk holden the siker weye;   1390
They been so knyt ther may noon harm bityde,
And namely upon the wyves syde.
For which this Januarie, of whom I tolde,
Considered hath inwith his dayes olde
The lusty lyf, the vertuous quyete   1395
That is in mariage hony-sweete;
And for his freendes on a day he sente
To tellen hem th' effect of his entente.
   With face sad his tale he hath hem toold.
He seyde, "Freendes, I am hoor and oold,   1400
And almoost, God woot, on my pittes brynke;
Upon my soule somwhat moste I thynke.
I have my body folily despended;
Blessed be God that it shal been amended!
For I wol be, certeyn, a wedded man,   1405
And that anoon in al the haste I kan.
Unto som mayde fair and tendre of age,
I prey yow, shapeth for my mariage
Al sodeynly, for I wol nat abyde;
And I wol fonde t'espien on my syde   1410

To whom I may be wedded hastily.
But forasmuche as ye been mo than I,
Ye shullen rather swich a thyng espyen
Than I, and where me best were to allyen.
    But o thyng warne I yow, my freendes deere,
I wol noon oold wyf han in no manere.   1416
She shal nat passe twenty yeer, certayn;
Oold fissh and yong flessh wolde I have ful fayn.
Bet is," quod he, "a pyk than a pykerel,
And bet than old boef is the tendre veel.   1420
I wol no womman thritty yeer of age;
It is but bene-straw and greet forage.
And eek thise olde wydwes, God it woot,
They konne so muchel craft on Wades boot,
So muchel broken harm whan that hem leste,   1425
That with hem sholde I nevere lyve in reste.
For sondry scoles maken sotile clerkis:
Womman of manye scoles half a clerk is.
But certeynly a yong thyng may men gye,
Right as men may warm wex with handes plye.
Wherfore I sey yow pleynly in a clause,   1431
I wol noon oold wyf han right for this cause.
For if so were I hadde swich myschaunce
That I in hire ne koude han no plesaunce,
Thanne sholde I lede my lyf in avoutrye,   1435
And go streight to the devel whan I dye.
Ne children sholde I none upon hire geten;
Yet were me levere houndes had me eten,
Than that myn heritage sholde falle
In straunge hand, and this I telle yow alle.
I dote nat, I woot the cause why   1441
Men sholde wedde, and forthermoore woot I
Ther speketh many a man of mariage
That woot namoore of it than woot my page,
For whiche causes man sholde take a wyf.   1445
If he ne may nat lyven chaast his lyf,
Take hym a wyf with greet devocioun,
By cause of leveful procreacioun
Of children, to th'onour of God above,
And nat oonly for paramour or love;   1450
And for they sholde leccherye eschue,
And yelde hir dette whan that it is due;
Or for that ech of hem sholde helpen oother

In meschief, as a suster shal the brother,
And lyve in chastitee ful holily.   1455
But sires, by youre leve, that am nat I.
For, God be thanked! I dar make avaunt,
I feele my lymes stark and suffisaunt
To do al that a man bilongeth to;
I woot myselven best what I may do.   1460
Though I be hoor, I fare as dooth a tree
That blosmeth er that fruyt ywoxen bee;
And blosmy tree nys neither drye ne deed.
I feele me nowhere hoor but on myn heed;
Myn herte and alle my lymes been as grene
As laurer thurgh the yeer is for to sene.   1466
And syn that ye han herd al myn entente,
I prey yow to my wyl ye wole assente."
    Diverse men diversely hym tolde
Of mariage manye ensamples olde.   1470
Somme blamed it, somme preysed it, certeyn;
But atte laste, shortly for to seyn,
As al day falleth altercacioun
Bitwixen freendes in disputisoun,
Ther fil a stryf bitwixe his bretheren two,   1475
Of whiche that oon was cleped Placebo,
Justinus soothly called was that oother.
    Placebo seyde, "O Januarie brother,
Ful litel nede hadde ye, my lord so deere,
Conseil to axe of any that is heere,   1480
But that ye been so ful of sapience
That yow ne liketh, for youre heighe prudence,
To weyven fro the word of Salomon.
This word seyde he unto us everychon:
'Wirk alle thyng by conseil,' thus seyde he,
'And thanne shaltow nat repente thee.'   1486
But though that Salomon spak swich a word,
Myn owene deere brother and my lord,
So wysly God my soule brynge at reste,
I holde youre owene conseil is the beste.   1490
For, brother myn, of me taak this motyf,
I have now been a court-man al my lyf,
And God it woot, though I unworthy be,
I have stonden in ful greet degree
Abouten lordes of ful heigh estaat;   1495
Yet hadde I nevere with noon of hem debaat.

I nevere hem contraried, trewely;
I woot wel that my lord kan moore than I.
With that he seith, I holde it ferme and stable;
I seye the same or elles thyng semblable.   1500
A ful greet fool is any conseillour
That serveth any lord of heigh honour
That dar presume or elles thenken it
That his conseil sholde passe his lordes wit.
Nay, lordes been no fooles, by my fay!   1505
Ye han youreselven shewed heer to-day
So heigh sentence, so holily and weel,
That I consente and conferme everydeel
Youre wordes alle and youre opinioun.
By God, ther nys no man in al this toun,   1510
Ne in Ytaille, that koude bet han sayd!
Crist halt hym of this conseil ful wel apayd.
And trewely, it is an heigh corage
Of any man that stapen is in age
To take a yong wyf; by my fader kyn,   1515
Youre herte hangeth on a joly pyn!
Dooth now in this matiere right as yow leste,
For finally I holde it for the beste."
     Justinus, that ay stille sat and herde,   1519
Right in this wise he to Placebo answerde:
"Now, brother myn, be pacient, I preye,
Syn ye han seyd, and herkneth what I seye.
Senek, amonges othere wordes wyse,
Seith that a man oghte hym right wel avyse
To whom he yeveth his lond or his catel.   1525
And syn I oghte avyse me right wel
To whom I yeve my good awey fro me,
Wel muchel moore I oghte avysed be
To whom I yeve my body for alwey.
I warne yow wel, it is no childes pley   1530
To take a wyf withouten avysement.
Men moste enquere, this is myn assent,
Wher she be wys, or sobre, or dronkelewe,
Or proud, or elles ootherweys a shrewe,
A chidestere, or wastour of thy good,   1535
Or riche, or poore, or elles mannysh wood.
Al be it so that no man fynden shal
Noon in this world that trotteth hool in al,
Ne man ne beest swich as men koude devyse;

But nathelees it oghte ynough suffise 1540
With any wyf, if so were that she hadde
Mo goode thewes than hire vices badde;
And al this axeth leyser for t'enquere.
For, God it woot, I have wept many a teere
Ful pryvely syn I have had a wyf. 1545
Preyse whoso wole a wedded mannes lyf,
Certein I fynde in it but cost and care
And observances, of alle blisses bare.
And yet, God woot, my neighebores aboute,
And namely of wommen many a route, 1550
Seyn that I have the mooste stedefast wyf,
And eek the mekeste oon that bereth lyf;
But I woot best where wryngeth me my sho.
Ye mowe, for me, right as yow liketh do;
Avyseth yow—ye been a man of age— 1555
How that ye entren into mariage,
And namely with a yong wyf and a fair.
By hym that made water, erthe, and air,
The yongeste man that is in al this route
Is bisy ynough to bryngen it aboute 1560
To han his wyf allone. Trusteth me,
Ye shul nat plesen hire fully yeres thre,—
This is to seyn, to doon hire ful plesaunce.
A wyf axeth ful many an observaunce.
I prey yow that ye be nat yvele apayd." 1565
    "Wel," quod this Januarie, "and hastow sayd?
Straw for thy Senek, and for thy proverbes!
I counte nat a panyer ful of herbes
Of scole-termes. Wyser men than thow,
As thou hast herd, assenteden right now 1570
To my purpos. Placebo, what sey ye?"
    "I seye it is a cursed man," quod he,
"That letteth matrimoigne, sikerly."
And with that word they rysen sodeynly,
And been assented fully that he sholde 1575
Be wedded whanne hym liste and where he wolde.
    Heigh fantasye and curious bisynesse
Fro day to day gan in the soule impresse
Of Januarie aboute his mariage.
Many fair shap and many a fair visage 1580
Ther passeth thurgh his herte nyght by nyght,
As whoso tooke a mirour, polisshed bryght,

And sette it in a commune market-place,
Thanne sholde he se ful many a figure pace
By his mirour; and in the same wyse   1585
Gan Januarie inwith his thoght devyse
Of maydens whiche that dwelten hym bisyde.
He wiste nat wher that he myghte abyde.
For if that oon have beaute in hir face,
Another stant so in the peples grace   1590
For hire sadnesse and hire benyngnytee
That of the peple grettest voys hath she;
And somme were riche and hadden badde name.
But nathelees, bitwixe ernest and game,
He atte laste apoynted hym on oon,   1595
And leet alle othere from his herte goon,
And chees hire of his owene auctoritee;
For love is blynd alday and may nat see.
And whan that he was in his bed ybroght,
He purtreyed in his herte and in his thoght
Hir fresshe beautee and hir age tendre,   1601
Hir myddel smal, hire armes longe and sklendre,
Hir wise governaunce, hir gentillesse,
Hir wommanly berynge, and hire sadnesse.
And whan that he on hire was condescended,   1605
Hym thoughte his choys myghte nat ben amended.
For whan that he hymself concluded hadde,
Hym thoughte ech oother mannes wit so badde
That inpossible it were to repplye
Agayn his choys: this was his fantasye.   1610
His freendes sente he to, at his instaunce,
And preyed hem to doon hym that plesaunce
That hastily they wolden to hym come;
He wolde abregge hir labour, alle and some.
Nedeth namoore for hym to go ne ryde;   1615
He was apoynted ther he wolde abyde.
    Placebo cam and eek his freendes soone,
And alderfirst he bad hem alle a boone,
That noon of hem none argumentes make   1619
Agayn the purpos which that he hath take,
Which purpos was plesant to God, seyde he,
And verray ground of his prosperitee.
    He seyde ther was a mayden in the toun,
Which that of beautee hadde greet renoun,

Al were it so she were of smal degree; 1625
Suffiseth hym hir yowthe and hir beautee.
Which mayde, he seyde, he wolde han to his wyf,
To lede in ese and hoolynesse his lyf;
And thanked God that he myghte han hire al
That no wight his blisse parten shal. 1630
And preyed hem to laboure in this nede,
And shapen that he faille nat to spede;
For thanne, he seyde, his spirit was at ese.
"Thanne is," quod he, "no thyng may me displese,
Save o thyng priketh in my conscience, 1635
The which I wol reherce in youre presence.
    I have," quod he, "herd seyd ful yoore ago,
Ther may no man han parfite blisses two,—
This is to seye, in erthe and eek in hevene.
For though he kepe hym fro the synnes sevene,
And eek from every branche of thilke tree, 1641
Yet is ther so parfit felicitee
And so greet ese and lust in mariage,
That evere I am agast now in myn age
That I shal lede now so myrie a lyf, 1645
So delicat, withouten wo and stryf,
That I shal have myn hevene in erthe heere.
For sith that verray hevene is boght so deere
With tribulacion and greet penaunce,
How sholde I thanne, that lyve in swich pleasaunce 1650
As alle wedded men doon with hire wyvys,
Come to the blisse ther Crist eterne on lyve ys?
This is my drede, and ye, my bretheren tweye,
Assoilleth me this question, I preye."
    Justinus, which that hated his folye, 1655
Answerde anon right in his japerye;
And for he wolde his longe tale abregge,
He wolde noon auctoritee allegge,
But seyde, "Sire, so ther be noon obstacle
Oother than this, God of his hygh myracle
And of his mercy may so for yow wirche 1661
That, er ye have youre right of hooly chirche,
Ye may repente of wedded mannes lyf,
In which ye seyn ther is no wo ne stryf.
And elles, God forbede but he sente 1665
A wedded man hym grace to repente

Wel ofte rather than a sengle man!
And therefore, sire—the beste reed I kan—
Dispeire yow noght, but have in youre memorie,
Paraunter she may be youre purgatorie! 1670
She may be Goddes meene and Goddes whippe;
Thanne shal youre soule up to hevene skippe
Swifter than dooth an arwe out of a bowe.
I hope to God, herafter shul ye knowe
That ther nys no so greet felicitee 1675
In mariage, ne nevere mo shal bee,
That yow shal lette of youre savacion,
So that ye use, as skile is and reson,
The lustes of youre wyf attemprely,
And that ye plese hire nat to amorously, 1680
And that ye kepe yow eek from oother synne.
My tale is doon, for my wit is thynne.
Beth nat agast herof, my brother deere,
But lat us waden out of this mateere.
The Wyf of Bathe, if ye han understonde, 1685
Of mariage which we have on honde,
Declared hath ful wel in litel space.
Fareth now wel. God have yow in his grace."
   And with this word this Justyn and his brother
Han take hir leve and ech of hem of oother. 1690
For whan they saughe that it moste nedes be,
They wroghten so by sly and wys tretee
That she, this mayden, which that Mayus highte,
As hastily as evere that she myghte,
Shal wedded be unto this Januarie. 1695
I trowe it were to longe yow to tarie
If I yow tolde of every scrit and bond
By which that she was feffed in his lond,
Or for to herknen of hir riche array.
But finally ycomen is the day 1700
That to the chirche bothe be they went
For to receyve the hooly sacrement.
Forth comth the preest with stole aboute his nekke,
And bad hire be lyk Sarra and Rebekke
In wysdom and in trouthe of mariage; 1705
And seyde his orisons, as is usage,
And croucheth hem, and bad God sholde hem blesse,
And made al siker ynogh with hoolynesse.
   Thus been they wedded with solempnitee,

And at the feeste sitteth he and she 1710
With othere worthy folk upon the deys.
Al ful of joye and blisse is the paleys,
And ful of instrumentz and of vitaille,
The mooste deyntevous of al Ytaille.
Biforn hem stoode instrumentz of swich soun
That Orpheus, ne of Thebes Amphioun, 1716
Ne maden nevere swich a melodye.
At every cours thanne cam loud mynstralcye,
That nevere tromped Joab for to heere,
Nor he Theodomas, yet half so cleere, 1720
At Thebes whan the citee was in doute.
Bacus the wyn hem shynketh al aboute,
And Venus laugheth upon every wight,
For Januarie was bicome hir knyght,
And wolde bothe assayen his corage 1725
In libertee and eek in mariage;
And with hire fyrbrond in hire hand aboute
Daunceth biforn the bryde and al the route.
And certeinly, I dar right wel seyn this,
Ymeneus, that god of weddyng is, 1730
Saugh nevere his lyf so myrie a wedded man.
Hoold thou thy pees, thou poete Marcian,
That writest us that ilke weddyng murie
Of hire Philologie and hym Mercurie,
And of the songes that the Muses songe! 1735
To smal is bothe thy penne and eek thy tonge
For to descryven of this mariage.
Whan tendre youthe hath wedded stoupyng age,
Ther is swich myrthe that it may nat be writen.
Assayeth it youreself, thanne may ye witen
If that I lye or noon in this matiere. 1741
    Mayus, that sit with so benyngne a chiere,
Hire to biholde it semed fayerye.
Queene Ester looked nevere with swich an ye
On Assuer, so meke a look hath she. 1745
I may yow nat devyse al hir beautee,
But thus muche of hire beautee telle I may,
That she was lyk the brighte morwe of May,
Fulfild of alle beautee and plesaunce.
    This Januarie is ravysshed in a traunce 1750
At every tyme he looked on hir face;

But in his herte he gan hire to manace
That he that nyght in armes wolde hire streyne
Harder than evere Parys dide Eleyne.
But nathelees yet hadde he greet pitee   1755
That thilke nyght offenden hire moste he,
And thoughte, "Allas! O tendre creature,
Now wolde God ye myghte wel endure
Al my corage, it is so sharp and keene!
I am agast ye shul it nat susteene.   1760
But God forbede that I dide al my myght!
Now wolde God that it were woxen nyght,
And that the nyght wolde lasten everemo.
I wolde that al this peple were ago."
And finally he dooth al his labour,   1765
As he best myghte, savynge his honour,
To haste hem fro the mete in subtil wyse.
    The tyme cam that resoun was to ryse;
And after that men daunce and drynken faste,
And spices al aboute the hous they caste,   1770
And ful of joye and blisse is every man,—
Al but a squyer highte Damyan,
Which carf biforn the knyght ful many a day,
He was so ravysshed on his lady May   1774
That for the verray peyne he was ny wood.
Almoost he swelte and swowned ther he stood,
So soore hath Venus hurt hym with hire brond,
As that she bar it daunsynge in hire hond;
And to his bed he wente hym hastily.
Namoore of hym as at this tyme speke I,   1780
But there I lete hym wepe ynogh and pleyne,
Til fresshe May wol rewen on his peyne.
    O perilous fyr that in the bedstraw bredeth!
O famulier foo that his servyce bedeth!
O servant traytour, false hoomly hewe,   1785
Lyk to the naddre in bosom sly untrewe,
God shilde us alle from youre aqueyntaunce!
O Januarie, dronken in plesaunce
In mariage, se how thy Damyan,
Thyn owene squier and thy borne man,   1790
Entendeth for to do thee vileynye.
God graunte thee thyn hoomly fo t'espye!
For in this world nys worse pestilence

Than hoomly foo al day in thy presence. 1794
    Parfourned hath the sonne his ark diurne:
No lenger may the body of hym sojurne
On th 'orisonte as in that latitude.
Night with his mantel that is derk and rude
Gan oversprede the hemysperie aboute;
For which departed is this lusty route 1800
Fro Januarie, with thank on every syde.
Hoom to hir houses lustily they ryde,
Where as they doon hir thynges as hem leste,
And whan they sye hir tyme, goon to reste.
Soone after that, this hastif Januarie 1805
Wolde go to bedde, he wolde no lenger tarye.
He drynketh ypocras, clarree, and vernage
Of spices hoote t'encreessen his corage;
And many a letuarie hath he ful fyn,
Swiche as the cursed monk, daun Constantyn,
Hath writen in his book *De Coitu*; 1811
To eten hem alle he nas no thyng eschu.
And to his privee freendes thus seyde he:
"For Goddes love, as soone as it may be,
Lat voyden al this hous in curteys wyse." 1815
And they han doon right as he wol devyse.
Men drynken, and the travers drawe anon.
The bryde was broght abedde as stille as stoon;
And whan the bed was with the preest yblessed,
Out of the chambre hath every wight hym dressed; 1820
And Januarie hath faste in armes take
His fresshe May, his paradys, his make.
He lulleth hire, he kisseth hire ful ofte;
With thikke brustles of his berd unsofte,
Lyk to the skyn of houndfyssh, sharp as brere—
For he was shave al newe in his manere— 1826
He rubbeth hire aboute hir tendre face,
And seyde thus, "Allas! I moot trespace
To yow, my spouse, and yow greetly offende
Er tyme come that I wil doun descende. 1830
But nathelees, considereth this," quod he,
"Ther nys no werkman, whatsoevere he be,
That may bothe werke wel and hastily;
This wol be doon at leyser parfitly.
It is no fors how longe that we pleye; 1835

In trewe wedlok coupled be we tweye;
And blessed be the yok that we been inne,
For in oure actes we mowe do no synne.
A man may do no synne with his wyf,
Ne hurte hymselven with his owene knyf;   1840
For we han leve to pleye us by the lawe."
Thus laboureth he til that the day gan dawe;
And thanne he taketh a sop in fyn clarree,
And upright in his bed thanne sitteth he,   1844
And after that he sang ful loude and cleere,
And kiste his wyf, and made wantown cheere.
He was al coltissh, ful of ragerye,
And ful of jargon as a flekked pye.
The slakke skyn aboute his nekke shaketh   1849
Whil that he sang, so chaunteth he and craketh.
But God woot what that May thoughte in hir herte
Whan she hym saugh up sittynge in his sherte,
In his nyght-cappe, and with his nekke lene;
She preyseth nat his pleyyng worth a bene.
Thanne seide he thus, "My reste wol I take;
Now day is come I may no lenger wake."   1856
And doun he leyde his heed and sleep til pryme.
And afterward, whan that he saugh his tyme,
Up ryseth Januarie; but fresshe May   1859
Heeld hire chambre unto the fourthe day,
As usage is of wyves for the beste.
For every labour somtyme moot han reste,
Or elles longe may he nat endure,
This is to seyn, no lyves creature,
Be it of fyssh, or bryd, or beest, or man.   1865
    Now wol I speke of woful Damyan
That langwissheth for love, as ye shul heere;
Therfore I speke to hym in this manere:
I seye, "O sely Damyan, allas!
Andswere to my demaunde as in this cas.   1870
How shaltow to thy lady, fresshe May,
Telle thy wo? She wole alwey seye nay.
Eek if thou speke, she wol thy wo biwreye.
God be thyn helpe! I kan no bettre seye."
    This sike Damyan in Venus fyr   1875
So brenneth that he dyeth for desyr,
For which he putte his lyf in aventure.

No lenger myghte he in this wise endure,
But prively a penner gan he borwe,
And in a lettre wroot he al his sorwe, 1880
In manere of a compleynt or a lay,
Unto his faire, fresshe lady May;
And in a purs of sylk, heng on his sherte
He hath it put and leyde it at his herte. 1884
 The moone, that at noon was thilke day
That Januarie hath wedded fresshe May
In two of Tawr, was into Cancre glyden;
So longe hath Mayus in hir chambre abyden,
As custume is unto thise nobles alle.
A bryde shal nat eten in the halle 1890
Til dayes foure, or thre dayes atte leeste,
Ypassed been; thanne lat hire go to feeste.
The fourthe day compleet fro noon to noon,
Whan that the heighe masse was ydoon,
In halle sit this Januarie and May, 1895
As fressh as is the brighte someres day.
And so bifel how that this goode man
Remembred hym upon this Damyan,
And seyde, "Seynte Marie! how may this be,
That Damyan entendeth nat to me? 1900
Is he ay syk, or how may this bityde?"
His squieres, whiche that stooden ther bisyde,
Excused hym by cause of his siknesse,
Which letted hym to doon his bisynesse; 1904
Noon oother cause myghte make hym tarye.
 "That me forthynketh," quod this Januarie,
 "He is a gentil squier, by my trouthe!
If that he deyde, it were harm and routhe.
He is as wys, discreet, and as secree
As any man I woot of his degree, 1910
And therto manly and eek servysable,
And for to been a thrifty man right able.
But after mete, as soone as evere I may,
I wol myself visite hym, and eek May,
To doon hym al the confort that I kan." 1915
And for that word hym blessed every man
That of his bountee and his gentillesse
He wolde so conforten in siknesse
His squier, for it was a gentil dede. 1919

"Dame," quod this Januarie, "taak good hede,
At after-mete ye with youre wommen alle,
Whan ye han been in chambre out of this halle,
That alle ye go se this Damyan.
Dooth hym disport—he is a gentil man;
And telleth hym that I wol hym visite,   1925
Have I no thyng but rested me a lite;
And spede yow faste, for I wole abyde
Til that ye slepe faste by my syde."
And with that word he gan to hym to calle
A squier that was marchal of his halle,   1930
And tolde hym certeyn thynges what he wolde.
   This fresshe May hath streight hir wey yholde
With alle hir wommen unto Damyan.
Doun by his beddes syde sit she than,
Confortynge hym as goodly as she may.   1935
This Damyan, whan that his tyme he say,
In secree wise his purs and eek his bille,
In which that he ywriten hadde his wille,
Hath put into hire hand, withouten moore,
Save that he siketh wonder depe and soore,
And softely to hire right thus seyde he: 1941
"Mercy! and that ye nat discovere me,
For I am deed if that this thyng be kyd."
This purs hath she inwith hir bosom hyd,
And wente hire wey; ye gete namoore of me.
But unto Januarie ycomen is she,   1946
That on his beddes syde sit ful softe.
He taketh hire and kisseth hire ful ofte,
And leyde hym doun to slepe, and that anon.
She feyned hire as that she moste gon   1950
Ther as ye woot that every wight moot neede;
And whan she of this bille hath taken heede,
She rente it al to cloutes atte laste,
And in the pryvee softely it caste.
   Who studieth now but faire fresshe May?
Adoun by olde Januarie she lay,   1956
That sleep til that the coughe hath hym awaked.
Anon he preyde hire strepen hire al naked;
He wolde of hire, he seyde, han som plesaunce,
And seyde hir clothes dide hym encombraunce,

And she obeyeth, be hire lief or looth. 1961
But lest that precious folk be with me wrooth,
How that he wroghte I dar nat to yow telle;
Or wheither hire thoughte it paradys or helle.
But heere I lete hem werken in hir wyse 1965
Til evensong rong, and that they moste aryse,
   Were it by destynee or aventure,
Were it by influence or by nature,
Or constellacion, that in swich estaat
The hevene stood, that tyme fortunaat 1970
Was for to putte a bille of Venus werkes—
For alle thyng hath tyme, as seyn thise clerkes—
To any womman for to gete hire love,
I kan nat seye; but grete God above,
That knoweth that noon act is causelees, 1975
He deme of al, for I wole holde my pees.
But sooth is this, how that this fresshe May
Hath take swich impression that day
Of pitee of this sike Damyan,
That from hire herte she ne dryve kan 1980
The remembrance for to doon hym ese.
"Certeyn," thoghte she, "whom that this thyng displese
I rekke noght, for heere I hym assure
To love hym best of any creature, 1984
Though he namoore hadde than his sherte."
Lo, pitee renneth soone in gentil herte!
   Heere may ye se how excellent franchise
In wommen is whan they hem narwe avyse.
Som tyrant is, as ther be many oon,
That hath an herte as hard as any stoon, 1990
Which wolde han lat hym sterven in the place
Wel rather than han graunted hym hire grace;
And hem rejoysen in hire crueel pryde,
And rekke nat to been an homycide.
   This gentil May, fulfilled of pitee, 1995
Right of hire hand a lettre made she,
In which she graunteth hym hire verray grace.
Ther lakketh noght, oonly but day and place,
Wher that she myghte unto his lust suffise;
For it shal be right as he wole devyse. 2000
And whan she saugh hir tyme upon a day,

To visite this Damyan gooth May,
And sotilly this lettre doun she threste
Under his pilwe, rede it if hym leste.
She taketh hym by the hand and harde hym twiste   2005
So secrely that no wight of it wiste,
And bad hym been al hool, and forth she wente
To Januarie whan that he for hire sente.
   Up riseth Damyan the nexte morwe:
Al passed was his siknesse and his sorwe.   2010
He kembeth hym, he preyneth hym and pyketh,
He dooth al that his lady lust and lyketh;
And eek to Januarie he gooth as lowe
As evere dide a dogge for the bowe.
He is so plesant unto every man   2015
(For craft is al, whoso that do it kan)
That every wight is fayn to speke hym good;
And fully in his lady grace he stood.
Thus lete I Damyan aboute his nede,
And in my tale forth I wol procede.   2020
   Somme clerkes holden that felicitee
Stant in delit, and therfore certeyn he,
This noble Januarie, with al his myght,
In honest wyse, as longeth to a knyght,
Shoop hym to lyve ful deliciously.   2025
His housynge, his array, as honestly
To his degree was maked as a kynges.
Amonges othere of his honeste thynges,
He made a gardyn, walled al with stoon;
So fair a gardyn woot I nowher noon.   2030
For, out of doute, I verraily suppose
That he that wroot the Romance of the Rose
Ne koude of it the beautee wel devyse;
Ne Priapus ne myghte nat suffise,
Though he be god of gardyns, for to telle   2035
The beautee of the gardyn and the welle
That stood under a laurer alwey grene.
Ful ofte tyme he Pluto and his queene,
Proserpina, and al hire fayerye,
Disporten hem and maken melodye   2040
Aboute that welle, and daunced, as men tolde.
   This noble knyght, this Januarie the olde,
Swich deyntee hath in it to walke and pleye,

That he wol no wight suffren bere the keye,
Save he hymself; for of the smale wyket   2045
He baar alwey of silver a clyket,
With which, whan that hym leste, he it unshette.
And whan he wolde paye his wyf hir dette
In somer seson, thider wolde he go,   2049
And May his wyf, and no wight but they two;
And thynges whiche that were nat doon abedde,
He in the gardyn parfourned hem and spedde.
And in this wyse, many a murye day
Lyved this Januarie and fresshe May.
But wordly joye may nat alwey dure   2055
To Januarie, ne to no creature.
     O sodeyn hap! o thou Fortune unstable!
Lyk to the scorpion so deceyvable,
That flaterest with thyn heed whan thou wolt stynge;
Thy tayl is deeth thurgh thyn envenymynge.
O brotil joye! o sweete venym queynte!   2061
O monstre, that so subtilly kanst peynte
Thy yiftes under hewe of stidefastnesse,
That thou deceyvest bothe moore and lesse!
Why hastow Januarie thus deceyved,   2065
That haddest hym for thy fulle freend receyved?
And now thou hast biraft hym bothe his yen,
For sorwe of which desireth he to dyen.
     Allas! this noble Januarie free,
Amydde his lust and his prosperitee,   2070
Is woxen blynd, and that al sodeynly.
He wepeth and he wayleth pitously;
And therwithal the fyr of jalousie,
Lest that his wyf sholde falle in som folye,
So brente his herte that he wolde fayn   2075
That som man bothe hire and hym had slayn.
For neither after his deeth, nor in his lyf,
Ne wolde he that she were love ne wyf,
But evere lyve as wydwe in clothes blake,
Soul as the turtle that lost hath hire make.   2080
But atte laste, after a month or tweye,
His sorwe gan aswage, sooth to seye;
For whan he wiste it may noon oother be,
He paciently took his adversitee,
Save, out of doute, he may nat forgoon   2085

That he nas jalous everemoore in oon;
Which jalousye it was so outrageous,
That neither in halle n'yn noon oother hous,
Ne in noon oother place, neverthemo,
He nolde suffre hire for to ryde or go,   2090
But if that he had hond on hire alway;
For which ful ofte wepeth fresshe May
That loveth Damyan so benyngnely
That she moot outher dyen sodeynly,
Or elles she moot han hym as hir leste.   2095
She wayteth whan hir herte wolde breste.
    Upon that oother syde Damyan
Bicomen is the sorwefulleste man
That evere was; for neither nyght ne day
Ne myghte he speke a word to fresshe May,
As to his purpos of no swich mateere,   2101
But if that Januarie moste it heere,
That hadde an hand upon hire everemo.
But nathelees, by writyng to and fro,
And privee signes, wiste he what she mente,
And she knew eek the fyn of his entente.   2106
    O Januarie, what myghte it thee availle,
Thogh thou myghte se as fer as shippes saille?
For as good is blynd deceyved be
As to be deceyved whan a man may se.   2110
    Lo, Argus, which that hadde an hondred yen,
For al that evere he koude poure or pryen,
Yet was he blent, and, God woot, so been mo
That wenen wisly that it be nat so.
Passe over is an ese, I sey namoore.   2115
    This fresshe May that I spak of so yoore,
In warm wex hath emprented the clyket
That Januarie bar of the smale wyket,
By which into his gardyn ofte he wente;
And Damyan, that knew al hire entente,   2120
The cliket countrefeted pryvely.
Ther nys namoore to seye, but hastily
Som wonder by this clyket shal bityde,
Which ye shul heeren if ye wole abyde.   2124
    O noble Ovyde, ful sooth seystou, God woot,
What sleighte is it, thogh it be long and hoot,
That Love nyl fynde it out in som manere?

By Piramus and Tesbee may men leere:
Thogh they were kept ful longe streite overal,
They been accorded, rownynge thurgh a wal,   2130
Ther no wight koude han founde out swich a sleighte.
    But now to purpos: er that dayes eighte
Were passed, er the month of Juyn, bifil
That Januarie hath caught so greet a wil,   2134
Thurgh eggyng of his wyf, hym for to pleye
In his gardyn, and no wight but they tweye,
That in a morwe unto his May seith he:
"Rys up, my wyf, my love, my lady free!
The turtles voys is herd, my dowve sweete;
The wynter is goon with alle his reynes weete.   2140
Com forth now with thyne eyen columbyn!
How fairer been thy brestes than is wyn!
The gardyn is enclosed al aboute;
Com forth, my white spouse! out of doute
Thou hast me wounded in myn herte, O wyf!
No spot of thee ne knew I al my lyf.   2146
Com forth, and lat us taken oure disport;
I chees thee for my wyf and my confort."
    Swiche olde lewed wordes used he.
On Damyan a signe made she   2150
That he sholde go biforn with his cliket.
This Damyan thanne hath opened the wyket,
And in he stirte, and that in swich manere
That no wight myghte it se neither yheere,
And stille he sit under a bussh anon.   2155
    This Januarie, as blynd as is a stoon,
With Mayus in his hand, and no wight mo,
Into his fresshe gardyn is ago
And clapte to the wyket sodeynly.
    "Now wyf," quod he, "heere nys but thou and I,   2160
That art the creature that I best love.
For by that Lord that sit in hevene above,
Levere ich hadde to dyen on a knyf,
Than thee offende, trewe deere wyf!
For Goddes sake, thenk how I thee chees,   2165
Noght for no coveitise, doutelees,
But oonly for the love I had to thee.
And though that I be oold and may nat see,
Beth to me trewe, and I wol telle yow why.

Thre thynges, certes, shal ye wynne therby:
First, love of Crist, and to youreself honour,
And al myn heritage, toun and tour;   2172
I yeve it yow, maketh chartres as yow leste;
This shal be doon to-morwe er sonne reste,
So wisly God my soule brynge in blisse.   2175
I prey yow first in covenant ye me kisse;
And though that I be jalous, wyte me noght.
Ye been so depe enprented in my thoght
That, whan that I considere youre beautee,
And therwithal the unlikly elde of me,   2180
I may nat, certes, though I sholde dye,
Forbere to been out of youre compaignye
For verray love; this is withouten doute.
Now kys me, wyf, and lat us rome aboute."
   This fresshe May, whan she thise wordes herde,   2185
Benyngnely to Januarie answerde,
But first and forward she bigan to wepe.
"I have," quod she, "a soule for to kepe
As wel as ye, and also myn honour,
And of my wyfhod thilke tendre flour,   2190
Which that I have assured in youre hond,
Whan that the preest to yow my body bond;
Wherfore I wole answere in this manere,
By the leve of yow, my lord so deere:
I prey to God that nevere dawe the day   2195
That I ne sterve, as foule as womman may,
If evere I do unto my kyn that shame,
Or elles I empeyre so my name
That I be fals; and if I do that lak,
Do strepe me and put me in a sak,   2200
And in the nexte ryver do me drenche.
I am a gentil womman and no wenche.
Why speke ye thus? but men been evere untrewe,
And wommen have repreve of yow ay newe.
Ye han noon oother contenance, I leeve,   2205
But speke to us of untrust and repreeve."
   And with that word she saugh wher Damyan
Sat in the bussh, and coughen she bigan,
And with hir fynger signes made she
That Damyan sholde clymbe upon a tree   2210
That charged was with fruyt, and up he wente.

For verraily he knew al hire entente,
And every signe that she koude make,
Wel bet than Januarie, hir owene make;
For in a lettre she hadde toold hym al 2215
Of this matere, how he werchen shal.
And thus I lete hym sitte upon the pyrie,
And Januarie and May romynge ful myrie.
　　Bright was the day and blew the firmament;
Phebus hath of gold his stremes doun ysent,
To gladen every flour with his warmnesse. 2221
He was that tyme in Geminis, as I gesse,
But litel fro his declynacion
Of Cancer, Jovis exaltacion.
And so bifel, that brighte morwe-tyde, 2225
That in that gardyn in the ferther syde
Pluto, that is kyng of Fayerye,
And many a lady in his compaignye,
Folwynge his wyf, the queene Proserpyna,
Which that he ravysshed out of Ethna 2230
Whil that she gadered floures in the mede—
In Claudyan ye may the stories rede
How in his grisely carte he hire fette—
This kyng of Fairye thanne adoun hym sette
Upon a bench of turves, fressh and grene, 2235
And right anon thus seyde he to his queene:
　　"My wyf," quod he, "ther may no wight seye nay;
Th'experience so preveth every day
The tresons whiche that wommen doon to man.
Ten hondred thousand [tales] tellen I kan
Notable of youre untrouthe and brotilnesse.
O Salomon, wys and richest of richesse, 2242
Fulfild of sapience and of worldly glorie,
Ful worthy been thy wordes to memorie
To every wight that wit and reson kan. 2245
Thus preiseth he yet the bountee of man:
'Amonges a thousand men yet foond I oon,
But of wommen alle foond I noon.'
　　Thus seith the kyng that knoweth youre wikkednesse.
And Jhesus, *filius Syrak,* as I gesse, 2250
Ne speketh of yow but seelde reverence.
A wylde fyr and corrupt pestilence
So falle upon youre bodyes yet to-nyght!

Ne se ye nat this honurable knyght,   2254
By cause, allas! that he is blynd and old,
His owene man shal make hym cokewold.
Lo, where he sit, the lechour in the tree!
Now wol I graunten, of my magestee,
Unto this olde, blynde, worthy knyght
That he shal have ayen his eyen syght,   2260
Whan that his wyf wold doon hym vileynye.
Thanne shal he knowen al hire harlotrye,
Bothe in repreve of hire and othere mo."
    "Ye shal?" quod Proserpyne, "wol ye so?
Now by my moodres sires soule I swere   2265
That I shal yeven hire suffisant answere,
And alle wommen after for hir sake;
That, though they be in any gilt ytake.
With face boold they shulle hemself excuse,
And bere hem doun that wolden hem accuse.
For lak of answere noon of hem shal dyen.   2271
Al hadde man seyn a thyng with bothe his yen,
Yit shul we wommen visage it hardily,
And wepe, and swere, and chyde subtilly,
So that ye men shul been as lewed as gees.   2275
    What rekketh me of youre auctoritees?
I woot wel that this Jew, this Salomon,
Foond of us wommen fooles many oon.
But though that he ne foond no good womman,
Yet hath ther founde many another man   2280
Wommen ful trewe, ful goode, and vertuous.
Witnesse on hem that dwelle in Cristes hous;
With martirdom they preved hire constance.
The Romayn geestes eek make remembrance
Of many a verray, trewe wyf also.   2285
But, sire, ne be nat wrooth, al be it so,
Though that he seyde he foond no good womman,
I prey yow take the sentence of the man;
He mente thus, that in sovereyn bontee
Nis noon but God, but neither he ne she.   2290
    Ey! for verray God, that nys but oon,
What make ye so muche of Salomon?
What though he made a temple, Goddes hous?
What though he were riche and glorious?
So made he eek a temple of false goddis.   2295

How myghte he do a thyng that moore forbode is?
Pardee, as faire as ye his name emplastre,
He was a lecchour and an ydolastre,
And in his elde he verray God forsook;   2299
And if that God ne hadde, as seith the book,
Yspared him for his fadres sake, he sholde
Have lost his regne rather than he wolde.
I sette right noght, of al the vileynye
That ye of wommen write, a boterflye!
I am a womman, nedes moot I speke,   2305
Or elles swelle til myn herte breke.
For sithen he seyde that we been jangleresses,
As evere hool I moote brouke my tresses,
I shal nat spare for no curteisye   2309
To speke hym harm that wolde us vileynye."
    "Dame," quod this Pluto, "be no lenger wrooth;
I yeve it up! but sith I swoor myn ooth
That I wolde graunten hym his sighte ageyn,
My word shal stonde, I warne yow certeyn.
I am a kyng, it sit me noght to lye."   2315
    "And I," quod she, "a queene of Fayerye!
Hir answere shal she have, I undertake.
Lat us namoore wordes heerof make;
For sothe, I wol no lenger yow contrarie."
    Now lat us turne agayn to Januarie   2320
That in the gardyn with his faire May
Syngeth ful murier than the papejay,
"Yow love I best, and shal, and oother noon."
So longe aboute the aleyes is he goon
Til he was come agaynes thilke pyrie   2325
Where as this Damyan sitteth ful myrie
An heigh among the fresshe leves grene.
    This fresshe May, that is so bright and sheene,
Gan for to syke and seyde, "Allas, my syde!
Now sire," quod she, "for aught that may bityde,   2330
I moste han of the peres that I see,
Or I moot dye, so soore longeth me
To eten of the smale peres grene.
Help, for hir love that is of hevene queene!
I telle yow wel, a womman in my plit   2335
May han to fruyt so greet an appetit
That she may dyen, but she of it have."

"Allas!" quod he, "that I ne had heer a knave
That koude clymbe! Allas, allas," quod he,
"For I am blynd!" "Ye, sire, no fors," quod she;   2340
"But wolde ye vouche sauf, for Goddes sake,
The pyrie inwith youre armes for to take,
For wel I woot that ye mystruste me,
Thanne sholde I clymbe wel ynogh," quod she,
"So I my foot myghte sette upon youre bak."   2345
    "Certes," quod he, "theron shal be no lak,
Mighte I yow helpen with myn herte blood."
He stoupeth doun, and on his bak she stood,
And caughte hire by a twiste, and up she gooth—
Ladyes, I prey yow that ye be nat wrooth:
I kan nat glose, I am a rude man—   2351
And sodeynly anon this Damyan
Gan pullen up the smok, and in he throng.
    And whan that Pluto saugh this grete wrong,
To Januarie he gaf agayn his sighte,   2355
And made hym se as wel as evere he myghte.
And whan that he hadde caught his sighte agayn,
Ne was ther nevere man of thyng so fayn,
But on his wyf his thoght was everemo.
Up to the tree he caste his eyen two,   2360
And saugh that Damyan his wyf had dressed
In swich manere it may nat been expressed,
But if I wolde speke uncurteisly;
And up he yaf a roryng and a cry,   2364
As dooth the mooder whan the child shal dye:
"Out! help! allas! harrow!" he gan to crye,
"O stronge lady stoore, what dostow?"
    And she answerde, "Sire, what eyleth yow?
Have pacience and resoun in youre mynde!
I have yow holpe on bothe youre eyen blynde.
Up peril of my soule, I shal nat lyen,   2371
As me was taught, to heele with youre eyen
Was no thyng bet, to make yow to see,
Than strugle with a man upon a tree.
God woot, I dide it in ful good entente."   2375
    "Strugle!" quod he, "ye algate in it wente!
God yeve yow bothe on shames deth to dyen!
He swyved thee; I saugh it with myne yen,
And elles be I hanged by the hals!"
    "Thanne is," quod she, "my medicyne fals;

For certeinly, if that ye myghte se, 2381
Ye wolde nat seyn thise wordes unto me.
Ye han som glymsyng, and no parfit sighte."
    "I se," quod he, "as wel as evere I myghte,
Thonked be God! with bothe myne eyen two,
And by my trouthe, me thoughte he dide thee so." 2386
    "Ye maze, maze, goode sire," quod she;
"This thank have I for I have maad yow see.
Allas," quod she, "that evere I was so kynde!"
    "Now, dame," quod he, "lat al passe out of mynde. 2390
Com doun, my lief, and if I have myssayd,
God helpe me so as I am yvele apayd.
But, by my fader soule, I wende han seyn
How that this Damyan hadde by thee leyn,
And that thy smok hadde leyn upon his brest." 2395
    "Ye, sire," quod she, "ye may wene as yow lest.
But, sire, a man that waketh out of his sleep,
He may nat sodeynly wel taken keep
Upon a thyng, ne seen it parfitly,
Til that he be adawed verraily. 2400
Right so a man that longe hath blynd ybe
Ne may nat sodeynly so wel yse,
First whan his sighte is newe come ageyn,
As he that hath a day or two yseyn.
Til that youre sighte ysatled be a while, 2405
Ther may ful many a sighte yow bigile.
Beth war, I prey yow; for, by hevene kyng,
Ful many a man weneth to seen a thyng,
And it is al another than it semeth.
He that mysconceyveth, he mysdemeth." 2410
And with that word she leep doun fro the tree.
    This Januarie, who is glad but he?
He kisseth hire and clippeth hire ful ofte,
And on hire wombe he stroketh hire ful softe,
And to his palays hoom he hath hire lad. 2415
Now, goode men, I pray yow to be glad.
Thus endeth heere my tale of Januarie;
God blesse us, and his mooder Seinte Marie!

Epilogue

"Ey! Goddes mercy!" seyde oure Hooste tho,
"Now swich a wyf I pray God kepe me fro!

Lo, whiche sleightes and subtilitees   2421
In wommen been! for ay as bisy as bees
Been they us sely men for to deceyve,
And from the soothe evere wol they weyve;
By this Marchauntes tale it preveth weel.   2425
But doutelees, as trewe as any steel
I have a wyf, though that she povre be,
But of hir tonge, a labbyng shrewe is she,
And yet she hath an heep of vices mo;
Therof no fors! lat alle swiche thynges go.   2430
But wyte ye what? In conseil be it seyd
Me reweth soore I am unto hire teyd.
For, and I sholde rekenen every vice
Which that she hath, ywis, I were to nyce;
And cause why, it sholde reported be   2435
And toold to hire of somme of this meynee,—
Of whom, it nedeth nat for to declare,
Syn wommen konnen outen swich chaffare;
And eek my wit suffiseth nat therto,
To tellen al, wherfore my tale is do."   2440

Notes

For a detailed discussion of the important analogues to the *Merchant's Tale,*
see Germaine Dempster, "The *Merchant's Tale*," in *Sources and Analogues of
Chaucer's Canterbury Tales,* ed. W. F. Bryan and Germaine Dempster (New York,
1958), pp. 333–56.

1213   This line echoes the closing line of the *Clerk's Tale* immediately pre-
        ceding the *Merchant's Tale.*

1214   *on even and a-morwe:* evening and morning

1216   *trowe:* believe

1217   *woot:* know

1221   *What:* why

1222   *at al:* completely

1224   Griselde, a character in Chaucer's *Clerk's Tale,* is a model of wifely
        patience.

1226   *thee:* thrive

1227   *eft:* again

1230   Thomas is the "doubting Thomas" depicted in the Bible (*John* 20:24 ff.),
        not Thomas à Becket. According to legend, St. Thomas the Apostle
        preached in India.

1232   *shilde:* forbid

1236   *ryve:* pierce

1245   *Whilom:* once

1251   *seculeer:* laymen

1254   *corage:* desire, piety

1270   This image suggests both the commercial world and fruitfulness. The
        narrator and January view a wife as part of man's material possessions.

1277   *sit:* suits

1279   *brotel:* insecure

1280   *sikernesse:* security

1287   *buxom:* obedient

1288   *eek:* also

1292   *sterve:* die

1294   Theophrastus was the author of an antifeminist tract, *The Golden Book on Marriage.*

1295   *liste:* it please

1296   *housbondrye:* economy *plus* husbanding

1307   *sentence:* opinion

1313   *commune:* common rights

1314   *moebles:* movable goods

1320   *shent:* ruined

1325–32   The references to the Genesis story of Paradise adumbrate the later appearance of the serpent (Damian) in January's Edenic garden.

1335   *O flessh:* one flesh

1340–41   These lines may represent an oblique ironic allusion to two Biblical passages emphasizing the ineffable glory of heaven: *Isaiah* 64:4 and *I Cor.* 2:9.

1342   *swynke:* work

1350   *halt:* considers

1361   *rede:* advise

1362–74   The following Biblical allusions are *exempla* (often found in medieval sermon literature), stories which convey a moral truth and hence give the stamp of authority to a speaker's argument.

1363   Rebecca deceived her blind husband Isaac. See *Gen.* 27.

1366   For the Biblical story, see the apocryphal book of *Judith,* chaps. 11–13.

1369   See *I Sam.* 25:1-35.

1371   See *Esth.* 7.

1377   This line is derived from the *Distichs* of Dionysius Cato.

1384   For a lyrical depiction of Christ's devotion to the Church, see the *Song of Songs.*

1401   *pittes brynke:* the grave's edge

1410   *fonde:* strive

1424   Wade, a legendary hero, had a magic boat which allowed him to sail from place to place in a few minutes.

1429 *gye:* guide

1435 *avoutrye:* adultery

1461ff. In this striking tree image, January alludes to his white hair, symbolic of winter and old age; nevertheless, he claims that he has *grene lymes,* conventionally identified with spring, youth, and sexual potency.

1466 laurel, a symbol of fecundity and immortality.

1476 *Placebo* means "I will please." In the context of this tale, Placebo is an emblem of compliance and flattery.

1485–86 This quotation is actually derived from the apocryphal book of *Ecclesiasticus* 32:24 (Vulgate).

1523ff. See Seneca's *De Beneficiis,* chaps. 14–16.

1536 *mannysh wood:* "man-crazy," like the Wife of Bath

1538 The word *trotteth* evokes an image of horses. Like January, Justinus views women as material possessions.

1542 *thewes:* qualities

1565 *yvele apayd:* displeased

1568 *panyer:* basket

1580ff. The mirror image emphasizes January's erotic *fantasye:* his mind projects reality only in terms of his own sexual desires. Like merchandise *in a commune market-place,* young women as sexual wares pass by January's mirror.

1598 This proverbial expression emphasizes January's spiritual blindness and looks forward to his physical blindness.

1605 *condescended:* settled

1640–41 In medieval penitential literature, the Seven Deadly Sins were often depicted in terms of a tree with numerous branches. See, for example, Chaucer's *Parson's Tale.*

1646 *delicat:* delightful

1685 The Prologue to the *Wife of Bath's Tale* contains a lengthy discourse on marriage.

1697 *scrit:* deed

1698 *feffed:* put in possession

1704 The prayers in the Catholic marriage ceremony mention Sarah and Rebecca.

1707   *croucheth:* makes the sign of the cross over

1716   Orpheus, the famous Thracian musician of Greek legend, played his harp
       so sweetly that he charmed even wild beasts and birds; Amphion, another
       musician of Greek legend, helped by his magic lyre to construct a wall
       around Thebes.

1719   Joab blew a trumpet, thereby saving Israel (*II Sam.* 2).

1720   Thiodamas, an augur in the *Thebaid* of Statius, blew a trumpet of warn-
       ing whenever enemies attempted to besiege Thebes.

1722   Bacchus, god of wine and revelry.

1730   *Ymeneus:* Hymen

1732   Martianus Capella wrote a poem, *The Marriage of Philology and Mercury.*

1735   Muses, the nine patronesses of the arts in Greek mythology.

1744–45   See *Esth.* 5:2.

1750–54   The term *ravysshed,* underscored by the allusion to Paris and Helen
       of Troy, suggests the theme of abduction in the tale. Just as Paris'
       abduction of Helen caused the downfall of Troy, Damyan's betrayal of
       January and "abduction" of May leads to January's fall in the Edenic
       garden.

1762–63   These lines echo ironically a conventional theme found in the *aube*
       or dawn-song, a lyric farewell between lovers after a secret night spent
       together. See also ll. 1855–56.

1785   *hoomly hewe:* domestic servant

1810–11   Constantine Africanus, an eleventh-century monk and doctor, wrote *De
       Coitu.*

1835   *fors:* matter

1840   The phrase *his owene knyf* acquires a phallic association and is an ironic
       reminder of Damyan's role as January's carver. See also l. 2163.

1847   *ragerye:* passion

1881   complaint and lay, types of short poem.

1885–87   The moon has passed into Cancer from the second degree of Taurus
       through Gemini.

1953   *cloutes:* shreds

2029ff.   This beautiful garden, symbolically associated with the garden of love in
       the *Roman de la Rose,* the Garden of Eden, and the *hortus conclusus* (en-
       closed garden) in the *Song of Songs,* becomes the setting for adultery.

2032   The first part of the *Romance,* containing an allegorical garden, was com-
       posed by Guillaume de Lorris.

2034 Priapus, god of gardens, sex, and fertility.

2038–39 Pluto, the god of the underworld, abducted Proserpine in order to make her queen of the lower regions. The *fayerye* mentioned here more properly would be the entourage of a queen of the Celtic Otherworld than of Proserpine.

2046 *clyket:* small latch-key

2058 scorpion, conventional symbol of treachery.

2069 *free:* generous

2111 According to Greek legend, the hundred-eyed Argus was charged by Hera, the wife of Zeus, to watch over Io, Zeus's paramour. In spite of his hundred eyes, Argus was eventually deceived and killed by Hermes (Mercury).

2128 The story of Pyramus and Thisbe is found in Ovid's *Metamorphoses,* iv.

2138–48 These lines parody a number of verses from the *Song of Songs,* especially chaps. 2 and 4.

2163 *Levere:* rather

2217 *pyrie:* pear tree

2220 Phoebus Apollo, god of the sun.

2223–24 *declynacion:* time of least influence of a planet; *exaltacion:* time of greatest influence

2232 Claudian was the fourth-century author of *The Abduction of Proserpine.*

2247–48 See *Eccles.* 7:28.

2250 Jesus, the author of *Ecclesiasticus.*

2273 *visage:* face out

2275 *lewed:* ignorant

2300 See *I Kings* 11.

2336 The *fruyt* is reminiscent of the forbidden fruit in the Garden of Eden.

2374–76 The word *strugle* has a sexual connotation.

2378 *swyved:* had intercourse with

2400 *adawed:* awakened

2414 In "January's Caress" (*Lock Haven Review,* No. 10, 1968, pp. 3–6), Professor Rossell Hope Robbins argues convincingly for the identification of *wombe* with "queynte" (vulva). If his interpretation is correct, Chaucer's deft ironic touch is still present, for January's resurgence of sexual desire prompts him to *stroketh* (or *strikith*) May's *wombe* immediately after May has copulated with Damyan in the tree. If any child results from May's sexual union with Damyan and January, it will probably be Damyan's, and January, thinking the child to be his own, will still be the victim of *fantasye.*

2436   *meynee:* group

2438   *outen swich chaffare:* set out such wares

J. S. P. Tatlock

Chaucer's *Merchant's Tale**

For unrelieved acidity the *Merchant's tale* is approached nowhere in
Chaucer's works, and rarely anywhere else; it is one of the most sur-
prising pieces of unlovely virtuosity in all literature. Without a trace of
warm-hearted tolerance or genial humor, expansive realism or even
broadly smiling animalism, it is ruled by concentrated intelligence and
unpitying analysis. Its dexterity may be diverting to the reader, but that
is not the teller's mood. His utmost is to cast a lowering smile. There is
little of the external; none of that description of people's looks or dress
which is so brilliant in others of the bawdy tales, little of interior or out-
door scenes; even January's garden is vaguely dismissed—the author of
the *Romance of the rose* could not do it justice, nor Priapus himself (sug-
gestive deity).[1] Though the tale contains greater obscenity than any
other of the *Canterbury tales*, so much so that it beguiled a later obtuse
"editor" into the obscenest of the interpolations in the manuscripts, all
this sounds as if written in 1930, as if due to the kind of savagery which
makes one bite on a sore tooth; it serves as an insolently deliberate
counterirritant to the cruel feeling, and is neither easily humorous nor
rawly animal. The basal refinement of the speaker is shown by disclaim-
ers and apologies at the coarsest points.[2] One might feel half-ashamed
of so greatly enjoying so merciless a tale, and might balk at prolonged
analysis, if this did not end, as we shall see, in cheerfully detaching us
from the prevailing mood.

Though no direct source is known, the essentials of the same fantastic
plot are in more than a half-dozen tales from the fourteenth and fifteenth

---

* Reprinted from *Modern Philology*, XXXIII (May, 1936), 367–381 by permission
of The University of Chicago Press. ©1936 by The University of Chicago Press.
[1] Ll. 2031–35. The laurel is mentioned for the ironical back-allusion (ll. 2037, 1466),
and the spring merely as a likely resort for fairies (ll. 2039–41).
[2] Ll. 1810–11, 2350–51, 2362–63.

centuries, in Italian, High and Low German, Latin, French, English; no one of them enough nearer to Chaucer than the others to pass as the sole origin, unless (as noted by Varnhagen and Koch) that in the Italian *Novellino,* of the fourteenth century or earlier. The plot /368/ may well have been learned by word of mouth, even in more versions than one. But should anyone ask who taught the poet how to invest it with form and words, there is no answer.

Chaucer's attentive skill appears most of all in the characterization. This is less subtle than in some of the tales, and is outlined in bold, black strokes. While such little as exists in other versions of this story is chiefly of the woman, it is on the husband (much as Kittredge and Root intimate) that the teller expends most of his unloving care. January's advanced age, so far as we can see, is among the fresh additions to the story. While persons of far more than his sixty years were not at all uncommon in the Middle Ages, and while the mortality in excess of that of today was doubtless mostly in the early years of life, it is probable, since the strifes and strains of adult life began then from five to ten years earlier than now, that January was meant to seem a really old man. But here, considering the mood of the poem, was a difficulty. An old man whose young wife plays him false has always, it is true, been regarded as fair game for ridicule, and is so treated in the *Miller's tale;* but not a loving old man who has become blind, unless by the very hard-hearted. Therefore the sour narrator heads off any possible sympathy for January by a full-length portrait beginning in the fourth line of the poem.[3] That we must needs despise what should be pitiful fixes the mood. All his life he has been a lecher, described in rather gross terms, and the narrator professes uncertainty whether his belated desire for matrimony is due to religious motives or to dotage (1253). Indeed, were this a historical and not an imaginary narrative, one might well suspect that his success with his light-o'-loves had departed, and that his exhibit of repentance and his sudden enthusiasm about marriage were a briefly buoyant escape from humiliation and despair. Senile lechery seems to anybody repulsive, ridiculous at best. It is characteristic of him that his description of various kinds of women is in terms of things to eat, that it is when he is in bed that he thinks over his candidates for bride, and that he weds a woman of no rank whose chief points are her youth and alluring figure; although interest in receiving a dowry was quite frank in the Middle Ages, he submits instead to giving a strict marriage settlement, and this in spite of the skilful negotiations of his marriage /369/ brokers. He cannot get over the idea that sex is always humorous; he practices the sensual stare, identifies virtue and innocence with igno-

---

[3] Likewise the *Canon's Yeoman's tale* heads off sympathy from the priest-victim.

rance, evidently aspires to the thrill of training his bride to be knowing in Venus' school, can hardly repress his impatience, and finds intense pleasure in insincere sentimental compassion over what is in store for her.[4] His folly is even less spared than his self-indulgence. He is so determined that the facts about women, men, and life shall be as he wishes them to be that his toadies find it safe to lay it on with a trowel.[5] He seems to be one of the unfortunate inheritors of prosperity and adulation who believe that after a lifetime on the wrong path they can easily find and enjoy the right one. The point of momentary pathos where he would obtain the pears for May and cannot—"Allas, allas, that I am blynd!"— is instantly spoiled by his ridiculous posture, crouching with the tree in his arms, that he may prevent any lover from following, and that from his back she may climb up to her lover who is already there above (2339–49). His folly is due to his egotism, and it is on this that the most unerring delicate strokes are spent. Though he is superficially well bred,[6] in the two scenes where he consults his friends as to his marriage the asking of advice is shown, perhaps for the first time in literature, as motivated unconsciously but entirely by the itch to talk about one's own affairs. With portentous solemnity he announces his intentions, laps up Placebo's fulsome speech, can hardly sit through Justinus' counsel of caution and moderation, but at once turns again to Placebo. When he has settled on May, he thinks every other man's wit so bad that there can be no more to say, and when he next meets them he drops the veil and requests that none shall oppose him. The decision of the conferences naturally is that he shall marry whom and when he pleases. His egotism will not even die with him, for he is one of those spouses who desire for a young mate a lifelong widowhood. At the end he is deluded no more by May's presence of mind than by his own vanity which recoils from an unwelcome truth.[7] /370/

With so repulsive and fatuous a husband there was danger that a certain amount of sympathy would be turned to the faithless wife, the sort of danger Chaucer also anticipated in other poems. This was averted by making May not worse than January but hardly a person at all. No one can pity a lay-figure. She is scarcely described, rarely speaks, and before the end has not a thought or a feeling except the most obvious. Whatever traits she has are learned of only by inference, and neither deserve nor invite sympathy. We infer inevitably that she is mercenary, and are

---

[4] Ll. 1418–22; 1581, 1599; 1601–2, 1625–26, 1692, 1696–98, 2166; 1594; 1750–63, 1828–30.

[5] Ll. 1478–1518, 1916–19, 2066.

[6] Ll. 1766–67, 1813–15.

[7] Ll. 1399 ("With face sad his tale he hath hem toold") ; 1566ff. (" 'Wel!' quod this Januarie, 'and hastow sayd?' ") ; 1575–76, 1605–10, 1618–20, 1691–92, 2077–80.

so informed by hints; she is hypocritical enough to be a reasonably
good actress in playing the game with simpering blandness, as she sits
"with so benyngne a chiere," meeker than Queen Esther; that she accepts her lot with cold scorn is implied in other hints—God knew what
she thought when she saw her most filthy bargain caroling in his shirt,
and whether she thought his lovemaking paradise or hell, and later in
one breath she tearfully protests her fidelity and signs to Damian; that
she is sensual with normal stimulus is shown by her instant response to
Damian after only four days of marriage.[8] All possibility of glamor in
the *amour* is destroyed by the fact that the place she needlessly selects
for reading their first love letter is a privy, and that she tears it up and
throws it therein—another infallible indication of the mood intended
by the poet.[9] Whatever this tale is, it is not a love story. "Fresh" and
"benign" are the two words constantly used of her; that so blooming a
girl can be so unscrupulous is the bitterest stroke of all. She plays on the
not wholly infirm January's belated but sincere desire for an heir by the
silly pretense that her longing for the little green pears in early June is
the longing of pregnancy. Her tears, like her excuses, are ready on tap.[10]
She recalls such a portrayal of soulless sensuality as the figure of Astarte
in John Sargent's mural in the Boston Public Library.

Damian is even more of a paper doll. Possibly Chaucer disliked to
consort intimately even in imagination with sneaking people; he had
much to learn from some writers of today. Further, the personality of
January, which, together with the situation, is Chaucer's main interest,
stands out the better against an unfigured background; the /371/ technique here is not expansion but concentration. However little guilt attached, in the view of fashionable readers and writers in the later Middle
Ages, to the young woman who entered on a *mariage de convenance* and
took a lover, still less attached to him. But for Damian any interest or
sympathy is impossible. He goes through the motions expected in fashionable literature from a youth newly in love; he covets May at once,
takes to his bed, writes verses, as to the consummation of his desires
merely does as he is bid, and after the exposure leaves the exculpation
to May.[11] The timidity and lack of enterprise are here in plenty which
seem to have been so attractive to the masterful dame of the later Middle
Ages, at least to read about. We infer that he is good-looking and well
bred, but that is all. The male type which Chaucer elaborated with so

---

[8] Ll. 1270, 1696–98, 2172–74; 1742–45; 1851–54, 1964, 2187–2209; 1893, 1982–85.
[9] Ll. 1950–54.
[10] Ll. 1437–40, 1448–49, 2335–37; 2187.
[11] Ll. 1774, 1779, 1881, 2116–21, 2208–16, 2368–2410.

much sympathy in Troilus, and with tolerant amusement in Aurelius, could not be treated with more negligent indifference than here. His tricks of a dandy and his pleasantness to everyone read like a parody on Chaucer's earlier account of the ennobling effect on Troilus of his happy love. In the garden he is in the ludicrous posture of squatting under a bush to wait in safety from January's jealous hands and ears;[12] as with January and persons in other tales, so here, Chaucer heightens moral degradation by degrading physically. If in the *Franklin's tale* Chaucer had outgrown what is sometimes called the "conventions of courtly love," in the *Merchant's* he arrantly turned against them. Much water had flowed under the bridge since he wrote the *Troilus;* compared with these two tales, it reads like the work of a much younger and more inexperienced though comprehensive and potent spirit.

The only other human personalities in the tale are January's two friends, Placebo and Justinus. The former is merely the "yes-man," who flatters in order to serve his own ends, who perceives his patron's desires and gives corresponding advice, and affects indignation at the honest man who tells the truth. His name, of course, was then a familiar and clever joke; the first word of an antiphon in the vespers of the dead, *"Placebo Domino in regione viventium,"* it lent itself to a sour pleasantry, repeated by Chaucer's Parson and by the friar in the *Sumner's tale.* The extraordinary speech in which, before his patron /372/ and all, he glories in his methods and motives in flattering (1491–1505) must be taken merely as an example of a not rare medieval literary usage—the confession. Just as the soliloquy, hardly practiced in real life by sane people, was used by the Elizabethan playwright as a dramatic means of conveying essential and completely trustworthy information to the audience, so was the public confession used by medieval dramatic narrators. To say nothing of Jean de Meun and William Dunbar, Chaucer himself uses it with the Wife of Bath and the Canon's Yeoman, with the Pardoner and the Sumner's friar. We are by no means called upon to believe that all of these would in actual life have said all which they say. This self-exhibition of a flatterer is merely another specimen of the teller's slashing bitterness which sweeps far beyond the protagonists. Nothing defines the teller's feeling better than the fact that the sole human being in the poem to whom he gives his own power of attorney is the other friend, Justinus; the world-worn disillusioned who has not lost his internal peace, who has learned resignation by expecting little, and gives the wisest advice he thinks has any chance of being accepted. The best of his gibes from his own experience is that among the priv-

---

[12] Ll. 2011–17, 2155, 2208; *TC*, I, 1072–85; III, 1772–1806.

ileges of matrimony are its abundant opportunities for the virtue of
penitence (1665–67). The most sympathetic line in the whole poem in-
troduces his final reply to January:

> Justinus, which that hated his folye.

The only other composed and placid note in the poem is not among
men at all. January and May have their divine counterparts in Pluto
and Proserpina. It was doubtless Chaucer's unerring tact and taste which
led him to substitute this pair for the Lord God and St. Peter (as in the
Novellino), or Jove and Mercury or Venus (who figure elsewhere). It
was fitting in so gray a tale to choose not the bright Olympians but the
dusky gods of Hades. It is true that, to preserve a modern tone, he calls
them king and queen of *fairye*, following the practice of such popu-
larizers of the classic as the early English lay and ballad of Orfeo, but
Chaucer knew better. Proserpina is the tart feminist who to win equality
with man will use the most feminine of methods, and by all means has
the last word. The deceitful and the unfair in the feminine is indeed
eternal; heaven does not redress the balance of earth. This same solidar-
ity of women in unfairness to men had been /373/ hit off by Justinus in
his account of her women friends' championship of his own wife, whom
he himself can merely patiently endure (1550). Pluto, though he knows
it hopeless, gives January his chance, but to restore bodily sight is boot-
less when the eyes of the mind are darkened. He is the man of power
who tolerates with amusement and possibly a dash of admiration his
wife's irrational and immoral tactics, because he values peace more than
trivial victory. This is the only part of the poem where the sarcasms
approach good nature.

The alterations made by Chaucer in the plot, chiefly the addition of
all that precedes the blindness, mostly promote the characterization.
January's folly and egotism are exhibited by the conferences with
Placebo and Justinus;[13] the details of the legal preliminaries to the
marriage emphasize the bride's mercenary motive; those of the marriage
itself give opportunity for irony. Sara and Rebecca, held up in good
faith as models in the prayer *Deus qui potestate virtutis* in the nuptial
mass, one need not forget show their "wysdom and trouthe" in the book
of *Genesis*, the one in meanly driving away a husband's respectable
concubine and firstborn son, the other in deceiving a blind husband in
behalf of an equally deceitful child. Many additions to incident and
speech contribute to dramatic irony (of which Chaucer is one of the

---

[13] Incident and wording full of reminiscences of *Melibeus*, Deschamps' *Miroir de
mariage*, M. Capella's *De nuptiis*, and other works (on the use of the second throughout the *Merchant's tale*, see Lowes in *Modern philology*, VIII, 165–86).

masters in English),[14] to the harsh contrast between the realities and January's conscious expectations. Of the dramatic irony he is the sole victim. The most brilliant case has been recorded before—a "yong thynge" can be molded like warm wax in the hands, thinks January; he does not know the next appearance of warm wax will be in the hands of his own young thing, nor for what purpose—counterfeiting the garden key.[15] His shaky confidence in his own masculinity and his compassion for May prove misplaced; her actual sentiments are in keen contrast with what he expects in her.[16] As if to enforce fur- /374/ ther a different view of love from that which is so heartfelt in the *Troilus,* January himself unconsciously plays the part of Pandar to his own undoing in bringing the lovers together; though like a tyrant irritated for a moment by Damian's fancied neglect of him, his temporary elation, the cheap expansive kindliness of the gratified sensualist praised by his toadies, plays into the lover's hand. Damian need not fear that May will betray him.[17] The bodily blindness which smites January, and even the cure of it, are a mere nothing to his permanent mental blindness.[18] Until near the end there is no touch of humor without more than a touch of mordancy; no one who grasps the whole, no reader except an exceedingly casual one, can think it a piece of irresponsible amusement. But of the end one might so think. Here the full intensity of the bitterness seems to have evaporated, the strain needed to relax, as if one might as well make the best of things and helplessly laugh; and thus the complete triumph of May. But there is another justification for her triumph. The deep-down more than merely worldly meaning of the whole poem is the inexorable chastisement for stubborn shutting the eyes to facts, and with this sound if one-sided philosophy May is the true heroine, well adjusted to her particular world, which allows the male nothing better than the gray peace of Justinus and Pluto. Yet the harshness has hardly abated, and in a half-dozen spots toward the end is even heightened by a new clashing of emotions, the creeping-in of a little truly Chaucerian compassion for January.

Not the least of his satisfactions no doubt the writer found in the style, which completely fits the cold intelligence of the whole. Chaucer never

---

[14] G. C. Dempster, *Dramatic irony in Chaucer* (Stanford University, 1932); *Univ. of Calif. chronicle,* XXV, 213–15. Mrs. Dempster's sure and delicate analysis shows his chief predecessors with this device to be Boccaccio and the authors of the *fabliaux.* Little of the irony in this tale has escaped her keen eye (pp. 46–58); I omit most which she records. The most complete and careful collection and discussion of similar tales are in two forthcoming studies by her.

[15] Ll. 1429–30, 2117.

[16] Ll. 1458–66, 1752–61, 1807–12, 1851–54, 1964.

[17] Ll. 1898–1925, 1942–43.

[18] Ll. 1598, 2109–10.

wrote more brilliantly. Scarcely anywhere do we find so many of those
unified couplets, balanced and antithetical,[19] the force of which he had
learned from the Latin elegiac distich, the closed couplet of Ovid; which
the sixteenth century was to learn again from the same master, and
hand on to the seventeenth for developing—overdeveloping. The style,
and these couplets, were probably what most attracted /375/ the youthful Pope to paraphrase this congenial poem. In Chaucer they are an
occasional embellishment, the more forceful not only because used
merely when most fitting, but also because with him first appearing in
English. In the irony there is one peculiar practice, especially in the
grave exordium of the narrator, in which he affects as his own the pious
hopes and ridiculous optimisms which swarm in January's mind. Repeatedly the glaze of unreality seems too weak to hold in the powerful
feeling beneath. Ironic control is shattered by the direct blow or brazen
sneer. As to wedlock,

> "In this world it is a paradys";
> Thus seyde this olde knyght, that was so wys.
> To take a wyf it is a glorious thyng,
> And namely whan a man is oold and hoor.
> A wyf wol laste, and in thyn hous endure,—
> Wel lenger than thee list, paraventure.
> Justinus, which that hated his folye.
> Whan tendre youthe hath wedded stoupying age,
> There is swich myrthe that it may nat be writen.[20]

In meditatione sua exarsit ignis, et locutus est in lingua sua. One cannot
but picture a volcanic crater, the black rough floor burst now and again
by a spurt of white-hot lava. Further, the teller's bitterness is so intense
that it runs amuck at everything. The clergy, he implies, are no chaster
than the laity.[21] With such a married life to follow, religion itself is be-
mocked in the marriage rite (said to have made all secure enough—with
ceremonial), and the benediction of the nuptial bed, and high mass just
before Damian's successful wooing, and January expressing his lust in the
words of Solomon's Song, then commonly interpreted by the love of
Christ for his church—"olde lewed wordes," the narrator calls these
words of the Holy Ghost. He even—and this is hard to forgive him—

---

[19] This statement is based on an unpublished dissertation by Mrs. M. A. Hill, at
Stanford University, 1924, "A study of rhetorical balance in Chaucer," partly printed
in *PMLA*, XLII, 845–61; see also G. P. Shannon, "Grimald's heroic couplet," *ibid.,*
XLV, 532–42 (part of another Stanford University dissertation).

[20] Ll. 1265–66, 1268–69, 1317–18, 1655, 1738–39.

[21] Ll. 1251, 1322. As said elsewhere, I believe it an error to take these as implying
sincere praise of the clergy. But if, as is likely, the tale was originally intended as a
retort to the present *Shipman's* told by the Wife of Bath, sarcasms against the un-
chastity of the clergy were especially fitting.

compares January's roar (ridiculous word) on seeing the lovers in the
tree to a mother's cry over her dying child.[22] Nothing is sacred. The early
part is full of double meanings, and for- /376/ ward allusions which differ
from the dramatic irony only in not being directly attributed to the
characters.

> And namely whan a man is oold and hoor,
> Thanne is a wyf the fruyt of his tresor;

the best of his treasures, yes, but the mercenary wife was the product
of his treasure. A wife's submissiveness and attentions to her infirm
husband prove here to be only in appearance. The warnings of
Theophrastus, rejected with affected indignation by the narrator, are
fulfilled. A husband cannot be deceived who takes his wife's advice, but
can always boldly keep his head up; it is at the urging of May that they
follow Damian into the garden, and are there disgraced. The scriptural
heroines adduced as models were all deceivers of their men.[23] Throughout there is no end to this sort of thing. It seemed like *fayerye* to look
at May; at once her later fairy ally Proserpina comes to mind. The
narrator affects apprehensiveness lest she may reject and denounce Damian. Chaucer's "favorite line," the softly Italianate

> Pitee renneth soone in gentil herte,

appears in a connection, as has been said, which turns its milk of human
kindness sour; no one can suppose that Chaucer means sincerely to attribute to May any womanly tenderheartedness.[24] Most of these further
meanings come naturally to the reader, and, there is no reason to doubt,
were intended. There are no cheap surprises; all is close knit and prepared. In spite of all this, the narrator is by no means wholly in the grip
of an emotion, but is its master. With all his concentration he admits
slight impersonal touches of imposing decoration, even gusts of fresh
air from the open heavens, especially in the defining of times and in-
fluences by the movements of the planets;[25] also in mere glimpses of
ritual and stately festivity. In the combination of Christian language
and ceremonial with pagan mythology—Bacchus as January's butler,

[22] Ll. 1708, 1819, 1894, 2138–49, 2364–65.

[23] Ll. 1269–70, 1288–92 and 1381–82, 1294–1310 and 2172–74, 1356–58 and 2135, 1362–
74. Chaucer omits those who were not such, among these heroines in the books he had
been reading.

[24] Ll. 1743, 2039, etc.; 1872–74; 1986 (cf. 1995), 1987–94. E. Meyer seems to mistake
the teller's attitude toward May (*Stud. z. engl. philol.*, XLVIII, 138). Indeed pretty
much everyone who has judged the tale seems to the present writer to have gone astray
except only G. L. Kittredge.

[25] Ll. 1795–99, 1885–87, 1969–70, 2220–24.

Venus with her nuptial firebrand dancing, Pluto and Proserpina at large
in the garden—there is also something both Italian and /377/ delicately
fantastic,[26] as there is (though not so delicately) in the plot. All this
just saves the poet from any accusation of taking his story too seriously.

He chose an Italian setting. January was born and presumably lives in
Pavia, a little south of Milan, the old Lombard capital which Chaucer is
likely enough to have visited in 1378. We find the Italian custom of
siesta.[27] Damian has a characteristic Italian name, most familiar as that
of one of two early martyrs (Cosmas and Damian), Romans in one tradition, commemorated in the canon of the Roman mass and even the
medieval English; also as that of St. Peter Damian, Italian reformer of
the eleventh century. There were sex and even priapean elements in the
popular cult of San Damiano in Italy,[28] but it is impossible to say whether
Chaucer was aware of them, though we have noticed his mention of
Priapus. Justinus, Justyn, obviously is so named because, with him and
Placebo, *videbitis quid sit inter justum et impium,—videntur mihi ser-
mones tui boni et justi; justus* corresponding to the "righteous" of the
English Bible. Found elsewhere in the later empire, Justinus is the name
of various saints, but chiefly in Italy, and Giustino has long been a
characteristic and not rare Italian name. There is no reason to believe
that Chaucer learned the tale with an Italian locale; nor in his less
dignified tales does he habitually consider the original setting in choosing his own. He is prone to place the more homely near home, the most
romantic in remote climes, the sophisticated or fantastic sometimes in
the more familiar parts of Western Europe; for the *Merchant's*, Lom-
bardy is not inevitable, but is fitting enough. Several matters may have
made him think of Italy. The likeliest known source is in the Italian
Novellino (though localized nowhere). He may have had Boccaccio and
one of his peculiar veins in mind. Why did he name the young wife May
and the old husband January? May and December have been familiar in
modern times as nicknames for such a pair, but I find no sign of them
earlier than the /378/ sixteenth and seventeenth centuries, nor outside
England, and they may well be an altered derivative from the *Merchant's
tale* itself. Boccaccio's *Filocolo* is believed to have been familiar to him,
and contains the close analogue to the *Franklin's tale* which many be-

---

26 Ll. 1700–1721, 1819, 2192, 2242–52, 2282–2302; 1722–28, 1777–78, 2038–41, 2227–32.
There may be hints here from the *Roman de la rose* ("Soc. anc. t. franc.," ll. 3424–28) ;
Ovid *Metam.* iv. 758–59; x. 6, etc. At the end of *As you like it* and the *Tempest* there
is a like imaginative appearance of the gods at a wedding. On the survival of pagan
usages at weddings in Italy in early Christian times see J. W. Draper, *Intellect. devel.*
(New York, 1876), I, 359. It has been suggested that the sylphs in Pope's *Rape of the
lock* are a reminiscence from his familiarity with the *Merchant's tale*.
    27 Ll. 1926–28, 1956–57.
    28 G. J. Laing, *Survivals of Roman religion* (New York, 1931), p. 76.

lieve its source; here, it will be remembered, the task required of the lover is a garden in January blooming as in May. The garden which figures so largely in most versions of the fruit-tree story might well have caused Chaucer's mind to dart back to this May garden in January, and in Italy. Indeed, what frosty old January hopes for is a May garden blooming in himself. Finally, I would recall what I said long ago as to possible reminiscence from Boccaccio's juvenile *Ameto*. This has not been proved, let us say emphatically, but is in no way improbable, and should not be denied. One sometimes reminds himself that when a possible relation cannot be rigidly proved it may be wiser to suspend judgment than to deny it. There seems great likelihood that during Chaucer's visits of probably three or four months in Italy he would read many books which would be too costly to buy and carry back with him to England; this fact, and his remarkably retentive memory for what struck him, may explain certain of the resemblances in his works to Boccaccio's, including the *Decameron*, even after the lapse of years. The husband's old age is in no other version of the story[29] and in no subsidiary source, and, unlike his blindness, is needless in this plot. Nor are the loves of an aged man and a young woman at all common in the vast field of pre-Chaucerian narrative,[30] and so far as I /379/ see, if found at all, are mostly barely mentioned. But by no means so in *Ameto*. The most marked resemblance here is in the bedroom scenes and the nymph Agapes' account of her life (not

---

[29] Except that in two of the remoter he is elderly, a point in them both minor and inconsequential (Boccaccio, *Decam.*, VII, 9; *Comoedia Lydiae*, in E. du Méril, *Poésies inéd. du M.A.* [Paris, 1854], p. 370).

[30] The most detailed accounts are in the second and fifth of the probably sixth-century elegies attributed to one Maximianus, certainly known to Chaucer (ed. R. Webster, [Princeton, 1900]; Kittredge in *Amer. jour. of philol.*, IX, 84–85; Miss E. Rickert, *Mod. philol.*, XXIX, 266; Coffman, *Speculum*, IX, 250–53; the last, in his article on old age, not, it is true, in medieval stories, has nothing else relevant here); but the details, far coarser, are unlike Chaucer's. Jealous husbands abound in later medieval literature; I find them old (presented without detail) in the *lais* of *Yonec* and *Guigemar*, the *Comoedia Lydiae* (mentioned above, and see Faral in *Romania*, L, 321–85), and one of the twenty and more *chansons de malmariée* (which have little detail and coarseness; K. Bartsch, *Afr. Romanzen u. Pastour.* [Leipzig, 1870], p. 13). The 150–200 *fabliaux* are seldom as subtle even as this; husbands are rough and stupid, and sometimes jealous (have reason to be), but I find none shown as old, lovers need no such help; still less are there any details of senile love-making. In a dozen or two of the most familiar medieval collections of *fabulae*, *exempla*, anecdotes, and tales, mostly Latin, there are a good number of cases of the jealous husband and sometimes the familiar "triangle." I find the husband old in only four cases—in John of Capua's *Directorium hum. vitae* (no jealousy, no lover; Hervieux, *Fabul. lat.*, V, 233); in one or two tales in the *Dolopathos* and the *Septem sapientes*—*Gibbosi* (no lover), *Juvenis femina* (jealousy and lover); in *Gesta Romanorum*, cap. 121 (rich, old, jealous husband, lover but no *liaison*; ed. A. Keller). In no case is there amorous detail. Robinson serviceably refers to T. M. Chotzen's *Recherches sur ... Dafydd ab Gwilym* (Paris, 1927; see pp. 242, 244–46), Chaucer's Welsh contemporary, in whom and whose fellow-bards not only jealous husbands but old and feeble and rich ones figure; but is not this

the fruit-tree story, though not dissimilar) and in her rich old bride-groom's physical senility. His early lascivious life, his flatteries to his bride, his bent figure, prickly beard, lean and flabby neck, his endear-ments, his feebleness, and use of external means to rouse his ardor, and the extremely opposite emotions of groom and bride are alike in the two, though more memorable and repulsive in Boccaccio.[31] A man of observa-tion and imagination might have invented all this, as Boccaccio did—I am far from belittling this fact; yet so many of such recurrences are sur-prising if mere coincidence. It would not be hard to believe that the savagery of the *Merchant's tale* was a masculine Englishman's retort to the young Italian author's effeminate insincerity and sentimental volup-tuousness. Boccaccio was not yet the manful original genius he turned out later. In several ways we may be reminded of William Wycherley three centuries after Chaucer, especially in *The plain dealer*, and his attitude toward his contemporaries.

By this time, if not before, it will be granted that the *Merchant's tale* among Chaucer's works is anything but typical or characteristic. It would be confusing to compare it with works by Juvenal or Swift or Byron or Samuel Butler, or with De Maupassant's *Boule de suif*; but it has more of their spirit than of that of him for whom the epithets so usual as to be almost shopworn are tolerant, charitable, genial. Any pontifical explanation would be far too bold. To attribute the tale to /380/ some time of bitterness and disillusion in the poet's own life would be no wiser than Dowden's oversimple explanation of certain of Shak-spere's plays. Doubtless Chaucer at times had had in his proper person something of the feeling so vivid in the poem, but there is no reason to ascribe this here to anything but his active imagination. He may have been deceived as Argus was, but, as he says himself of this,

Passe over is an ese, I sey namoore.

Nor is the writing of such a tale for the Merchant called for by any-thing in the account of him in the general *Prologue*, nor sufficiently by

---

due to Dafydd's own paramour being forced to marry such a husband (*Dict. nat. biogr.*) —besides being outside Chaucer's field of knowledge? In this field the incongruities of amorous old men and young women seem not yet to have become vulgar cues for laugh-ter. In later times we find something in general similar, as in the Commedia dell'Arte, and (as Mr. E. D. Lyon shows me) in Hans Sachs; also in fifteenth-century England under Chaucer's influence (J. O. Halliwell, *Select minor poems of John Lydgate* [Percy Soc., 1840], pp. 27 ff.). I find none but very faint parallels in classical Latin, or in any other references adduced by the commentators. *Mch. T.* and *Ameto*, so far as I find, stand quite apart and alone. Chaucer is far from presenting a hackneyed situation.

[31] Magheri-Moutier (ed.), XV, 123-25; and see *Anglia*, XXXVII, 100–106. H. M. Cummings (*Indebtedness of Chaucer's works to . . . . Boccaccio* [Cincinnati, 1916], p. 36), in spite of his desire to be judicial and just, does not come to grips with the real point here.

his own prologue. An adequate dramatic introduction is afforded by
the account there of his disappointing first two months of marriage,
and by hostility to lustful clerics, aged lechers, and women who betray
merchant-husbands, excited by the *Wife of Bath's Prologue* and her intended telling of the present *Shipman's tale*. But there is nothing in
sight to make inevitable the telling by so composed a personage of so
ruthless a story, still less to explain Chaucer's writing it.

The best motive to think of is a purely literary one. Chaucer has no
more marked trait of manner than his varieties of tone, pitch, key,
mode—each fulfilled with equal ease and adequacy. No one word fits
perfectly; what is meant is his own attitude to a poem, his own emo-
tional reaction to its matter, degree of identification of himself with it,
and the kind of response which he desired from his readers. It is hard
to think of any narrative poet who approaches him in this sign of virtuosity. To confine ourselves to the *Canterbury tales*, the *Knight's tale*
is gallant and poetically decorative, but detached; the *Miller's, Reeve's,*
and *Sumner's* keen on the surface and light-heartedly animal; the
Shipman's more refined and worldly, more disillusioned; the *Man of
Law's* leisurely, imposing, and aloof, rhetorically rather than poetically
decorative; the *Prioress'* heartfelt and maternal; the *Nun's Priest's* full
of variety of tempo, and humorous enjoyment; the *Pardoner's* simple
yet full of deep insight, and matchless for uncanny mystery; the *Wife
of Bath's* subordinating romance to ethical clarity and grasp of personalities; the *Friar's* surface-satire but with darts of discernment; the
Clerk's slow and sympathetic, subordinating human reality to ideal
beauty; the *Squire's* romantic yet lifelike wall-painting; the *Franklin's*
an exquisite blend of reality and the ideal, of the mar- /381/ velous and
the homely; the *Second Nun's* entering with imaginative sympathy into
an ideal largely bygone even to Chaucer. We need not suppose that he
was often consciously on the hunt for an unpracticed mode; rather that
his informing instinct ever pushing on—

My besy gost, that thursteth alwey newe—

divined possibilities of fresh expression in each fresh matter. Thus the
Merchant's tale, like the *Shipman's* in refinement ending in grossness,
goes far beyond it in seriousness, disillusionment, imagination, hardly
restrained emotion. It expresses not at all Chaucer's everyday personality, and perhaps but little of his experience of life; it is a firm embodiment of a mood in the imagination. No doubt he thoroughly
enjoyed his savagery, for the unwontedness and the chance for irony
and brilliance; and its level of fantasy keeps the tale from being too far
out of character. The more its people alienate us from humanity, the
nearer it draws us to their versatile and kindly creator in admiration

and fellow-feeling. Therefore the last impression of the *Merchant's tale* is not repugnant. Cold makes us aware of warmth, and something purely acrid heightens the worth of his prevailing clemency. Chaucer did not unreflectingly follow a compelling temperament, but was aware of his course.

G. G. Sedgewick

The Structure of
*The Merchant's Tale**

There is nothing new in this paper except, perhaps, in the way of assemblage and emphasis.[1] Nevertheless, this sort of thing, if done better than it will now be done, might properly be excused. The Merchant and his performance figure largely in discussions of chronology, order, sources, and analogues of *The Canterbury Tales*; and all this, of course, is basic and invaluable. But, apart from a remarkable essay by Professor Tatlock,[2] there has been no really substantial examination of the poem's art, no full study of the object as in itself it really is—and that still remains, surely, a function of criticism. Besides, as one would expect, critics are still apt to fight shy of Chaucer's fabliaux or else to handle them in a discursive and gingerly way, although a good deal of the poet's maturest workmanship is to be found in that Latin Quarter of the arts. No doubt *The Merchant's Tale* makes strenuous demands on the maturity of its readers; but, equally without question, it ranks, both in substance and in form, among the very best and most original of Chaucer's works. One sign of rank is the fact that it is out of category. It uses a fabliau as part of its structure, but as a whole it isn't a fabliau at all; or if it is one, it is unique in its kind. In it are found, I believe, most known devices of satire; but in its total effect, it is unlike any other satire known to me. If, in the terribly hackneyed phrase, *Troilus and Criseyde* is the first "psychological novel," *The Merchant's Tale* may quite as justly be called the first psychological short story. In complexity of texture, like the Wife of Bath in person, it passes "hem of Ypres and of Gaunt." All these apparently facile generalizations, I am very sure, can be

---

* Reprinted from *University of Toronto Quarterly, XVII* (July, 1948), 337–345, by permission of University of Toronto Press.
[1] This paper was read at the Quebec meeting of the Royal Society of Canada (Section II) in May, 1947.
[2] "Chaucer's *Merchant's Tale*" (*Modern Philology*, XXXIII, 367–81).

supported by plenty of specific evidence; but the full demonstration must await other hands. This paper merely attempts to underline certain phases of Chaucer's workmanship as he handles what is often considered to be a "plot suited to the Hottentot," as an outraged scholar has called it.

Such an attempt is all the more desirable, I think, now that certain important and well-known seams of Chaucerian scholarship are pretty nearly worked out. It is very improbable indeed that we shall learn any more about the internal chronology of *The Canterbury Tales* or about the order of the fragments that remain. Whether we wish to or not, we *must* accept the text of the tales—at least the text of Groups D, E, and F —as it is now arranged, willingly or unwillingly, by all editors of the cycle. And there is no choice left but to accept the present order of the tales as Chaucer's final intention, and to leave aside, as irrelevant to lit- erary criticism, the problem of how the order was finally arrived at. Tatlock's essay, to which I /338/ have referred, does that, resting, as it naturally would do, on the argument which he himself did so much to develop. No doubt all students of Chaucer should know of his previous vicissitudes of purpose; but they are finally brought back to the whole affair of the Merchant—in the general *Prologue*, the link with *The Clerk's Tale*, and his own deliverance—just as they first read it before their faith was shaken, as it may have been, by the higher criticism. If there were only one manuscript instead of many, faith would never have been shaken at all, since all parts of the whole production, *as it now stands,* hang together perfectly well.

As corollary to all this, Kittredge's famous essay on "the Marriage Group" of tales must be accepted as generally authoritative, whatever minor modifications have to be made in his statement.[3] It is undeniably based on the facts of the text as it now stands, and must continue to stand, in all editions of Chaucer. Consequently we need not now consider the Merchant in his larger dramatic relations with the Wife of Bath and the Clerk who precede him and the Franklin who follows.

Unhappily, older scholarship has left behind some petrified survivals —to borrow a term from Chaucer grammar—which must be got out of the way, since they suggest doubt of the structural integrity of Chaucer's scheme. It has been said, for instance, that the tale is not consistent with the Merchant's portrait in the general *Prologue*. For this opinion there is no solid foundation.

The Merchant's portrait is one of the shortest of the series: it is not drawn in such minute detail as are many of the others, and the story he has to tell is not so definitely foreshadowed, so to speak, as in the case of the Knight, the Wife of Bath, the Pardoner, and the Clerk. It *could* be

---

[3] "Chaucer's Discussion of Marriage" (*Modern Philology*, IX, 453–67).

that the Merchant's portrait was written late; or it may (or may not) be that Chaucer was already planning, when he wrote it, to keep in reserve another dark horse, like the Canon's Yeoman and the Nun's Priest, for those surprise entries which he delighted in. It doesn't really matter much. But it is certainly clear that Chaucer didn't think highly of his Merchant from the very beginning. The fellow has the proper front of beard, hat, boots, and manner. But it is only a front. He is something of a pompous bore, forever talking about his "percentages": anyone who has lived through a Western real-estate boom recognizes the kind. Besides, it seems he is not above shady dealings "in exchange"; and he cloaks insolvency with a "stately" manner in the best tradition of trade. His name?—Chaucer hints that he did not bother to find out or remember; and (in no contradiction of Professor Manly's explanation of this fact[4]) it seems odd that the Merchant is the only character to be singled out for such a curt dismissal. In short, whether or not it was Chaucer's intention from the beginning, the Merchant of the general *Prologue* is presented as a person ripely ready for /339/ the *exposé* which does occur and which explodes, when the time comes, with startling suddenness. That too is not unfitting: in fact it is quite in accord with the doctrine of dramatic probability. You may make whatever guess you like about Chaucer's previous or undeveloped intentions. But if it be argued that harmony between portrait and tale is a matter of pure luck, I can only reply, in the old wisecrack, that for people who like that sort of thing, it is the sort of thing they like.

Two rather more obvious survivals of error are still extant in the notes of Skeat, Manly, and Robinson—one error in all three editions, the other in one. No names can carry greater authority; and the two errors are therefore the more disturbing. Both of them, I am certain, are due to a fixed determination to find in *The Merchant's Tale*, as it stands, evidence of an earlier stage of the cycle's development, and to assign the tale to another teller. The first of them revolves around the single word "seculeer" in line 1251:

> [he] folwed ay his bodily delyt
> On wommen, ther as was his appetyt,
> As doon thise fooles that been seculeer.

Apparently, Skeat set the heresy going. In his notes in the great edition of 1895, he seems to explain that word as referring to the "secular clergy" (parish priests), for he says "as distinguished from the monks and friars." He does not explain why he makes the distinction here, and

---

[4] J. M. Manly, *Some New Light on Chaucer* (New York, 1926), 200; *Chaucer's Canterbury Tales* (New York, 1928), 515. See also Robinson, *Chaucer's Complete Works* (Boston, 1933), 759.

consequently his interpretation of the passage is left rather obscure. Whatever Skeat meant, Manly and Robinson definitely agree that "seculeer," in this passage, refers to clerics who are not monks and friars; and, so their inference runs, the tale must have been meant originally for a member of the regular orders.

This gloss appears to me extraordinary. If, as we have supposed before, there were only one manuscript of the tales extant and if that manuscript ordered the text as we now must order it, whether we like to do so or not, how would an unspoiled reader interpret "seculeer"? To him it could refer to nothing else than to "laymen," as it usually does, and as it does in the other three cases listed in the concordance as certainly Chaucerian.[5] And the Merchant would be saying in effect: "the worthy knight behaved as do all these bachelor fools who are laymen—that is, who are not protected from sin by holy orders." It would never occur to that reader to conjure up some unknown cleric, whether secular or regular, as the Merchant's substitute. Nor is there any need to do so now. No matter when the tale was written or where it was once placed, there is no valid reason for supposing that it was ever intended for anybody but the Merchant. All this has been pointed out before by Dr. Germaine Dempster, but I think she is the only /340/ scholar who has done so.[6] I will not labour the argument further, except to say that the Merchant's reference to laymen as frailer than the clergy is in key with his ironic deference to religion throughout the tale. He may even be taking sarcastic flings both at the Clerk's chastity and at his own habitual licence.

In line with his gloss of "secular," Professor Manly believed that the tale was out of the Merchant's character. "The Tale itself," he said, "can hardly have been originally composed with the Merchant in mind as narrator—the detached tone of quiet irony is entirely unsuited to the Merchant and contrary to the tone of his Prologue; cf. especially ll. 1267–1390."[7] Anyone who knew Professor Manly hesitates to contradict him— quite apart from the respect due to his vast learning. But if this passage he refers to *is* read in the light of that prologue, it is hard to think of words more inappropriate than "detached" and "quiet": one would rather say "savagely self-involved" and "violent." Of course there can be no argument about matters of taste. But it is something of a relief to find

---

[5] One of these cases occurs seventy-one lines further on in *The Merchant's Tale,* at line 1322, where there can be no possible doubt of the meaning. In Robinson's text, the other two occur at VII, 3450 and X, 960. Four closely assembled instances of the word are to be found in *The Romaunt of the Rose* (6150, 6232, 6244, 6250) : all mean "lay." In a dubious passage of *The Romaunt of the Rose* (7173), the plural noun "seculers" apparently means "parish priests."

[6] "The Original Teller of the *Merchant's Tale*" (*Modern Philology,* XXXVI, 1–8).

[7] *Chaucer's Canterbury Tales* (New York, 1928), 596.

that passage elsewhere described as "bitterly ironical," which it is, or even as "blasphemous," which, as far as Chaucer is concerned, it certainly isn't. Not that Manly's strangely dubious terms cannot be accounted for. If the tale is ever read out of context, under the conviction that the Merchant was never meant to tell it, then it may sound far milder than a tale told by an angry and disillusioned man who is deeply involved in a situation similar to that he is describing. Such a difference constantly occurs in dramatic contexts. The Three Robbers story, for example, is one thing when it is excerpted in a short story anthology, and quite another as the Pardoner tells it. In the Merchant's place in the text, *which we must now accept*, we must always remember that he is uncontrolledly angry, and therefore that the tale must always be read as sharpened into his own mood.

In the Friar's word, this has been a long "preambulacioun." But in my opinion it has been necessary to clear the ground. We can now turn without distraction to the main structure.

Again and again one must insist that *The Merchant's Tale* cannot be properly read apart from his own prologue. First, he has been angered by the blatancy of the archiwyf of Bath, and next he has found the patience of the Clerk's Griselda quite "inportable." Griselda is a very far cry from that devil of a woman, the "shrewe at al," whom he lately married; he was a fool to get married in the first place; if he could be "unbounden," so help him heaven he would never again be caught in that trap. So runs his prologue. And anyone who reads it now may feel like adapting to his case a ribaldry of George Bernard Shaw:

> After two months of wedded bliss with her,
> He now could say, O death where is thy sting?

At such an outburst of agreeable sentiment, Harry Bailly is so surprised /341/ and delighted that he limits himself, most unusually, to only three lines of comment, as if in fear he would halt the Merchant's lava-flow: "let us learn about women from you," he says, in effect, to the volcano.

The tale proper begins with one of those swift outlines of situation which Chaucer manages so often with such unfailing skill: place, level of society, old fellow with a past who is now determined on marriage—

> Were it for hoolynesse or for dotage
> I kan nat seye.

And in that line the dominant note of irony is sounded at once. (It is well to remind ourselves in passing that January's "sixty-yeer of age" might be a good decade more if Chaucer were writing now: the Middle

Ages deflated the purchasing power of advancing years.) Then old January is allowed a few lines in which to speak for himself:

> "Noon oother lyf," seyde he, "is worth a bene;
> For wedlock is so esy and so clene,
> That in this world it is a paradys."

To which the Merchant adds a dryly bitter comment:

> Thus seyde this olde knyght that was so wys.

The next 130 lines—those that Manly mentions—are presented as musings of the Merchant, and develop the theme with extraordinary complexity; for it is possible to read the whole passage in four different voices, so to speak, which fuse into a voice that is both multiple and one. On the surface—barring the first six verses and a sour note here and there—these lines sound like a prothalamium as indeed they are: only one withdraws the term when one realizes the nature of the song. Naïve innocents have actually been known, I am told, to read the passage as a glorification of marriage. And if the imagined cleric of the editors were really uttering it, he *should*, as a cleric, intend it in that way. But after the whole introduction, and especially the six verses I have just spoken of, intelligence must listen otherwise. A generation ago, people of our time were rejoicing in a discovery which they called "the stream of consciousness" method in fiction. Well, here it is, under date of the thirteen-nineties. That glory song is really the stream which has been passing through the mind of January, the old fool who was so wise: he has been indulging in the ancient human habit of rationalizing himself into doing what he was going to do anyway. Five of those six verses of warning run as follows:

> And certeinly, as sooth as God is kyng,
> To take a wyf it is a glorious thyng,
> And namely whan a man is oold and hoor;
> Thanne is a wyf the fruit of his tresor.
> Thanne sholde he tak a yong wyf and a feir. . . .

This doctrine is *not* "so esy and so clene": in fact, it has the taint of January's malodorous mind. And once or twice, to keep you alerted to the situation, a sour note is sounded not too obtrusively: "your wife," the singer slyly hints, "is the most enduring of your possessions—she will last longer than you want her to, perhaps." /342/

But the actual speaker, the Merchant, must be heard also, in his own right; and he speaks in a sort of double-talk. From the mouth of a man to whom marriage has been a literal hell, you cannot expect either innocent praise or the sentimentality of an old dotard. His voice, in Robinson's word, is "bitterly ironic"; there is a savage sneer in the "heigh stil" of his eloquence; his fine words about marriage are really ironic curses extorted by the spectacle of an amorous fool whom he is about to expose. But beneath the obvious savagery runs an undercurrent of which he seems at best half-conscious: for the curses fall on himself as well as on January. The stream of consciousness we see flow by was the Merchant's own, two months ago. That is how he knows what is going on in old January's mind. Chaucer is making him speak as if in a mood of ugly reminiscence and self-loathing.

The great length of this four-toned passage is structurally justified, quite apart from the absorbing interest which the feminist controversy had for people of Chaucer's time. Those 130 lines firmly establish the twofold centre of the ensuing story. They furnish the intended double-single view of the dotage of January and the ugly temper of the Merchant who reveals it. The passage fairly compels the main narrative itself to come into its sordid being; and when the compulsion has been exerted, that narrative begins at once and goes on unchecked.

I have analysed these 130 lines at such length for a reason which should now be clear: they furnish the most elaborate sample of the complexity of texture which is a chief characteristic of *The Merchant's Tale*. Many elements in the piece, if not intricately fourfold as here, seem to have in them at least an ironic duplicity. It is astonishing to note how many of his favourite subjects and narrative tricks Chaucer throws to the Merchant as food for irony. For instance, as a good many commentators have noted, the process turns courtly love all "up-so-doun." Late in the tale, May insists she is "a gentil womman and no wenche"; but after one sight of Damian she had put all "daunger" aside shamelessly and announced that she loved him "best of any creature, Though he namoore hadde than his sherte." Against that the Merchant, and Chaucer, calmly juxtapose an elegant theme-song of the courtly tradition:

Lo, pitee renneth soone in gentil herte.

And at once the coarseness of this love-affair and the one that happened two months ago is starkly underlined. Likewise, Chaucer likes to blow an elaborate astrological bubble in order, as often, to prick it with comic effect. The Merchant too blows his bubble; and it bursts with an effect which Rabelais would have admired: Phoebus and the Gemini are called together to witness nothing more noble than a cuckoldry. Or, for one more example, we recall that the fate of Palamon and Arcite was transferred to high Olympus for settlement. But the Merchant, as Tatlock observes, chooses his gods from the underworld; and, what is more, they are transformed into the little mean dark people of folk-lore, sitting about on a bench /343/ of turf. Pluto and Proserpina become deities fit to witness and direct another case of the erotic blindness of men and the "passyng crueltee" of women: women are the same everywhere, the Merchant implies, whether in this world or the other. These three and other artistic playthings of his, Chaucer hands over to the Merchant, to be instruments of an irony directed first at January and then, unconsciously or half-consciously, at the Merchant himself.

In the midst of all this complexity you never lose sight of the centre of the story: everything converges on it. It is an unusual centre. You look at it as through bifocal glasses, seeing first, January, and secondly, the Merchant; and somehow, the two finally blend into one. Or, to put it another way, it is a case of seeing a blinded sensualist through the eyes of a sensualist who is awakened and embittered. The spectacle, it must be said, is not pretty, nor was it meant to be. The more clearly you see the one kind of amorist, the more you can guess, at least, about the other. And no character in fiction is more cruelly visible than January.

> . . . upright in his bed than sitteth he;
> And after that he sang ful loude and cleere,
> And kiste his wyf, and made wantown cheere.
> He was al coltish, ful of ragerye,
> And ful of jargon as a flekked pye.
> The slakke skin aboute his nekke shaketh
> While that he sang, so chaunteth he and craketh;
> But Got woot what that May thoughte in hire herte
> When she hym saugh up-sittynge in his sherte,
> In his nyght-cappe, and with his nekke lene.

There was to be no match for that visibility until Hogarth learned to draw. January singing! And the Merchant sang two months ago.

The spectacle suggests one of the books which Chaucer professes to have read. Into the Merchant's mouth, he puts quotations from *The Wisdom of the Son of Sirach* (he makes little dark Pluto quote him too), who said "Out of garments a moth, out of women wickedness." That is a passage the Merchant should have spotted, if he knew the *Wisdom* at first hand. And certainly, to his own instruction, he should not have missed one of that book's characteristic triple balances: "Three men my soul abhorreth, and I am greatly offended in their life: a poor man that is proud, a rich man that is a liar, and an old man that is a lecher." This might be a text for a moral discourse on January and the Merchant's quite proper attitude to him. But the Merchant himself, more audible than visible, doesn't come off so very much better in the end; for he bears a family resemblance to his victim. No doubt their stories are not parallel at many points. Probably the Merchant is not so old; certainly he has this solace of superiority over January that his eyes were opened and remained open. But there is a fundamental likeness in situation: both men, well on in years, have married wives who played them false. And to put it baldly, the choice is between grossly revolting sentimentality on one hand and, on /344/ the other, bitterness that has passed into loathing and even blasphemy. Those two choices, as Shakespeare likes to show, are closely akin. And Chaucer makes them into the two faces of the unity of a tale. True, the Merchant refused to dictate an autobiography like the Wife of Bath's. But, in his mood at the moment, what other story had he to tell?

One notable thing he has to his credit, in the frequently observed fact that no one has ever told a more original tale. Oddly enough it is likewise a dense mosaic of references, allusions, quotations; but the total effect is as richly new as the garments new-washed in *The Tempest*— though how dreadfully different the wash! Whatever sources Chaucer uses—his own *Tale of Melibee*, the *Mirror of Marriage*, the Song of Solomon, even the marriage ritual, or whatever else—all these take on a new colour. One aspect, however, of this originality has not been noted as often as others: that is, Chaucer's use of the fabliau. For *The Merchant's Tale* is not a fabliau, though it incorporates one into its structure. It is like no other of *The Canterbury Tales*—not even those which it might be expected to resemble: it is called a fabliau because there is no other convenient name. No source has ever been suggested, so I am told, in which the notorious Pear Tree story is given a local habitation in the feminist dispute; and in some details, that story itself underwent significant changes under Chaucer's hand. Heaven defend me from reading all its versions. But apparently the Pluto-Proserpina episode is Chaucer's addition; and Tatlock says that the ignoble hero of the story is pictured as an old man only in the *Decameron* version, which, in the opinion of most scholars, Chaucer had not read. Where he got the structural hint for mating two very different strains, no one knows. Surely he was quite capable of getting it all by himself: it is one of those associations that look easy once a genius has made it. The main point is that, in *The Merchant's Tale*, the well-worn fabliau provides an issue, both natural and logical, for a character and a situation which have already been devised. It therefore *looks* as if it had been specially minted for this occasion, taking on a new and "modern" colour. Just as, to repeat the parallel, the Three Robbers story is one thing within its context and another out of it. No other fabliau in Chaucer or elsewhere, as far as I know, is handled in such a way. Literary firms like Miller, Reeve and Company are quite satisfied with rough stories in and for themselves, and so are all customers (including Chaucer and many other respectable people) who sometimes care to deal in that sort of thing. In contrast, *The Merchant's Tale* is a sort of drama in which the Pear Tree story constitutes the last act.

Perhaps the best way to realize the structural use of this old fabliau is to compare the Merchant's whole performance with those of the Wife of Bath and the Pardoner—self-confessors, all three. I say "performance" advisedly, since the narrative which each tells is only one element in a larger plan. The Wife's long prologue is boldly autobiographical, and her story of the Loathly Lady is merely an exemplum, by way of coda, which /345/ emphasizes the substance of her argument. The Pardoner too is shamelessly revealing himself, and he embeds a grim exemplum in the exhibition of his tricks. But *The Merchant's Tale* is autobiographic only by implication; it professes to analyse an old fool's mind on the eve of an action which is concluded under the Pear Tree. Let me repeat: the fabliau provides the inevitable issue of everything that went before, and it is therefore more "dramatic" in its effect than anything in the other famous tales.

One other suggestion I should have liked to develop more fully since it belongs to an area in which my own special interest lies. It is this: the Merchant's performance, in minute detail and in general structure, is soaked in irony—irony in nearly every one of its known forms. Dr. Dempster's essay on this subject[8] is full of sensitive perceptions, but I believe that she might have made a bolder use of her own principles in their structural application. All who have ever listened to the Merchant sense his almost too insistently ironic tone, whether they find it detached and quiet or bitter and savage: irony is now the ingrained colour of his mind. Even more important, however, than the constant pressure of details, is the building of the performance as a whole. One body of ironic material in that structure Chaucer of course inherited from the fabliau itself, for a January-May story is primitively ironic in its own substance. On the central character of that story, the Merchant turns a hostile eye and hand: it isn't so much that we see January responsible for his own befuddlement as that we see the Merchant manipulating him to that end. In like manner we watch the magician Prospero moving the characters of *The Tempest* about like pieces on a chess-board—though, unlike the Merchant, Prospero is benevolent in purpose. A spectacle like that stirs in a spectator the profoundly moving sense known as dramatic irony. There is also a third aspect to the scene. For the master of the

---

8 *Dramatic Irony in Chaucer* (Stanford University Press, 1932), 46–58.

whole show stands behind the Merchant manipulating *him*—so that the puppet enlarges, clarifies, and completes his own destructive self-revelation. In sum, *The Merchant's Tale* has three ironic dimensions, as if it were a figure of circles, the first enclosed by the second and the second by the third. It would be hard to think of a structure in literature more original, elaborate, tightly composed.

Bertrand H. Bronson

Afterthoughts on
The Merchant's Tale*

"Above all things," wrote Kittredge fifty years ago, "we must avoid the error of those critics who treat the Merchant as if he were Chaucer. Here, if ever, it is vitally necessary to bear the drama in mind." This is because the Merchant has loaded his story with "savage and cynical satire." "He goes all lengths, for he is half-mad with rage and shame."[1] In the march of critics in general agreement with this point of view, two or three are conspicuous, and Tatlock perhaps most of all, in the vigor of his uncompromising analysis. Unapproached he finds the tale 'for unrelieved acidity": 'one of the most surprising pieces of unlovely virtuosity in all literature." In the teller's bitterness, he declares, "one cannot but picture a volcanic crater, the black rough floor burst now and again by a spurt of white-hot lava."[2] Later critics echo the sentiment. "In all literature," asks Patch, "is there any irony, I wonder, more savage than this?"[3] And Holman: 'one of the most savagely obscene, angrily embittered, pessimistic, and unsmiling tales in our language . . . such dark cynicism . . . the people are a collection of lost souls."[4]

The critics who react in this way agree that the temper of the tale is not at all characteristic of gentle, tolerant Chaucer. Tatlock, in his wide-ranging familiarity with the spirit of the Middle Ages, judges that its like is scarcely to be found elsewhere; and he is driven to paradox in order to explain it. "The more its people," he says, "alienate us from humanity, the nearer it draws us to their versatile and kindly creator in

---

* Reprinted from *Studies in Philology*, LVIII (October, 1961), 583–596, by permission of the author and The University of North Carolina Press.
[1] G. L. Kittredge, *Chaucer and his Poetry* (1915), p. 202.
[2] J. S. P. Tatlock, "Chaucer's *Merchant's Tale*," *MP*, XXXIII (1935–6), 367–81.
[3] H. R. Patch, *On Rereading Chaucer* (1939), p. 228.
[4] C. H. Holman, "Courtly Love in the Merchant's and the Franklin's Tales," *ELH*, XVIII (1951), 241–52.

admiration and fellow-feeling . . . Cold makes us aware of warmth, and something purely acrid heightens the worth of his prevailing clemency."[5] But this, surely, is desperate pleading, and rather increases the wonder than tends to allay our questions. Why, we continue to ask, should Chaucer /584/ have been swept so far from his normal course on this one occasion, and nowhere else? If it is so foreign to his nature, should we not look for a better explanation? Is it possible that we have been misreading it? Are we perhaps so deeply imbued with our nineteenth-century inheritance that we do not see the tale as Chaucer's first audience would have received it, and as he himself may have meant it? Are we taking it as if it were an early version of Nabokov's *Laughter in the Dark?*

It is common knowledge that in approximately half of the more complete MSS of the Canterbury Tales, there is no Merchant's Prologue. The Merchant's Tale comes between the Squire's Tale and that of the Wife of Bath. It must, therefore, have been known to many in Chaucer's day and later without the explosive charge; and it is an unforced assumption that the Prologue and the Tale were composed at different times.

Except perhaps in the emphasis I intend to give it, this is familiar ground. In the great edition of 1894, Skeat wrote in his spacious way: "It is easy to see that Chaucer may have had a good deal of material in hand before the idea of writing a connected series of tales occurred to him. . . . His design [thenceforward] was to make a collection of tales which he had previously written, to write more new tales to go with these, and to unite them all into a series by means of connecting links. . . . In doing this, he did not work continuously, but inserted the connecting links as they occurred to him."[6] The existence of nine unconnected groups is by itself a signal of his way of working; and it is besides fairly evident that, with few and late exceptions, the tales were habitually written before their proper prologues. We have, too, the occasional clear marks of a change of intention, as in the Shipman's Tale and that of the Second Nun.

The repeated allusion to "secular" folk, in the Merchant's Tale, was not lost on earlier students, and years ago Manly suggested that the piece might have been intended for the Monk.[7] Later, Baugh entered the Friar a candidate for the same office.[8] It is no strain to believe that the Tale was in existence before it was assigned to its present teller. /585/

---

5 Tatlock, loc. cit.

6 W. W. Skeat, *Works of Geoffrey Chaucer* (1894, imp. 1926), III, 374–75.

7 J. M. Manly (ed), *Chaucer's Canterbury Tales* (1928), p. 624.

8 A. C. Baugh, "The Original Teller of the Merchant's Tale," *MP*, XXXV (1937), 15–26.

In a cogent essay, Sedgewick has given short shrift to scholarly musings about the way things might once have been. He dubs these "petrified survivals" and turns with contempt from the game of hypotheses. Our guesses about "Chaucer's previous or undeveloped intentions" are, he declares, a waste of time. From other quarters we have recently heard minatory warnings against the "intentional fallacy." Sedgewick says, we must accept the text as it now stands arranged by all the editors, and "leave aside, as irrelevant to literary criticism," problems of antecedent conditions.[9]

But in spite of current distaste, there may be something still to be learned from circumspect efforts to recover the state of mind in which Chaucer beat out his works at the creative forge. Nothing is more certain than that scholarship, like other mundane activities, follows fashions; and that when the dark luminary of Irony, under whose countenance our critics now steal, has reached its zenith, it must begin to decline. We need not be disheartened if we are old-fashioned: Victorianism is already in the ascendant!

I am not concerned here to revive a hypothesis that Chaucer had initially intended the Merchant's Tale for another pilgrim. I wish to climb still farther upstream. What I think has gone too long unheeded, and what therefore I should like briefly to explore, is the literary or artistic corollary of the admission that the Merchant's Tale was composed before and independent of the Merchant's Prologue. If we are to try to recover the spirit in which the Tale was written, we must first endeavor to erase from our minds, in reading it, all traces of whatever we have learned from the Merchant's Prologue, from that source alone. Accepting for the present what the "inedited" MSS tell us by their headings, that the Tale without the Prologue had been *assigned* to the Merchant, we are led back for information about the teller to the General Prologue, which we must suppose already extant by that time. From the General Prologue two facts can be extracted. One is, that the Merchant and the Clerk were conceived and set side by side as a contrasting pair, in life and in philosophy. The other is negative: that when the Merchant was first drawn Chaucer had not yet divined that his private life was a witches cauldron of marital bitterness and disillusion. The grounds of the anticipated oppo- /586/ sition between Merchant and Clerk were then materialism *vs.* idealism. Their difference lay not at all in conflicting views of marriage and its promise of weal or woe but in an all-embracing world-outlook of opposing values. The stories, when they came, would presumably illustrate these radical oppositions in one

---

[9] G. G. Sedgewick, "The Structure of *The Merchant's Tale*," *UTQ*, XVII (1948), 337–45.

way or another. And so they do: the carrion, shall we say, lying by the violet in the sun, corrupting with virtuous season.

But since we want to regain Chaucer's starting-point as creative artist, we must, I think, do more, and with some sweet oblivious antidote cleanse our memories of the Merchant altogether. We must approach the Tale as it was in the beginning, unrelated to any dramatic rôle whatever of a character assumed. And this ought not to prove impossible, for on close inspection there is not one of the pilgrims of whom we can say that this tale is particularly suitable to him. Postponing questions of psychological propriety, and searching within the tale for objective clues to a physical way of life, marks of a profession, or level of culture, we find singularly little to assist us. The speaker calls himself "a rude man," which suggests that he is acquainted with refinement, as does his professed wish to avoid uncourteous language. At that point in his story he is self-conscious about the crudeness of his subject-matter, and apologizes to the ladies in his audience—but who are they? We may be sure the Nuns were out of earshot, and the Wife of Bath was not in the least squeamish: "I nam nat precius," she expressly declares. Chaucer must have been thinking of a more courtly audience,—doubtless the one in front of him—and, by the same token, of himself. Consciousness of audience appears at other points: for example, in the line, "But lest that precious folk be with me wrooth . . . I dar nat to yow telle"; and in "Asseyeth it youreself"; and in the characteristically Chaucerian "I trowe it were to longe yow to tarie," a mark of oral delivery but otherwise unindicative.

The teller appears to have some familiarity with high life and perhaps a certain appreciation of wealth and luxury. He is clearly an educated man with an interest in learning and literature. Classical and biblical allusions are frequent, and a number of ancient authors are invoked by name. It is noticeable that he has access to the same books as clerk Jankyn, Dame Alice's fifth husband. Possibly the two had met erstwhile in Chaucer's library. /587/ He knows something about medicine and medical literature, and obviously has acquaintance with astronomy. The two notorious allusions to "secular" folk are to my mind not revealing. "As doon thise fooles that been seculeer" means simply, lay persons who are fools to boot; and the other signifies only that those who are not safe in the arms of the Church are better off married. But it may be presumed as well that, not to mention the clerical persons among the Pilgrim audience, there would be a sprinkling of Churchmen, noble or notable, in the company to which Chaucer was reading. A gesture in their direction could do no harm.

It may also be inferred that the company addressed was an habitual one for Chaucer, one with whom he felt he could take liberties of speech,

whose tastes he knew, and among whom he was at ease. They stimulated
him, we can hardly doubt, to do his best—or worst, if you are not "secular"—and their ready appreciation must have instigated the more
unbridled parts of the Canterbury Tales. They followed his work as it
grew, and remembered it. This is proved by Justinus' unparalleled allusion to the Wife of Bath's excursus on marriage. Chaucer was obviously
counting here on his company's delighted recollection of a probably
recent reading, for otherwise they would be left out of the joke, and the
reference, since it goes unexplained, would be pointless and mystifying.
But it is solely intended for them,—not for the persons in the Tale—
and the poet, in high confidence of appreciative recognition, cared not
in the least about the breach of verisimilitude. Dramatic it is, unquestionably; but Realism? the devil go therewith!

We can hardly disagree with Tatlock's interpretation of the relevant
details as leading to an assured conclusion that the Melibeus, the Wife's
Prologue, and the Merchant's Tale were written closely together, probably in that order. There are too many points of connection to leave
room for doubt. The many parallel passages between the Melibeus and
the Tale prove that the latter is sometimes demonstrably a poetic paraphrase, without intermediary, of Chaucer's own prose; and that over all
even the plot and characterization of the Tale have been affected by the
tract.[10] And again, there is between the Wife's Prologue and the tale of
January a parallel citation of authorities seldom mentioned elsewhere
in /588/ Chaucer's work. Here and there, also, there are lines in common. The strategy of introducing an opposite argument by quotation,
ostensibly to condemn it but effectually to assert it, is followed in both
pieces, though to be sure on a contrary course. The destination, however,
is the same. Two passages, seldom exhibited side by side, gain enormously
by juxtaposition and also epitomize the basically desperate character
of the underlying debate:

(The Wife)   Upon a nyght, Jankyn, that was oure sire,
              Redde on his book, as he sat by the fire,
              Of Eva first, that for hir wikkednesse
              Was al mankynde broght to wrecchednesse,
              For which that Jhesu Crist hymself was slayn,
              That boghte us with his herte blood agayn.
              Lo, heere expres of womman may ye fynde,
              That womman was the los of al mankynde. [D 713 ff]

(Merchant)   And herke why I sey nat this for noght,
              That womman is for mannes helpe ywroght.

---

[10] J. S. P. Tatlock, *The Development and Chronology of Chaucer's Works* (1907),
p. 215.

> The hye God, whan he hadde Adam maked,
> And saugh him al allone, bely-naked,
> God of his grete goodnesse seyde than,
> "Lat us now make an helpe unto this man
> Lyk to hymself"; and thanne he made him Eve.
> Heere may ye se, and heerby may ye preve,
> That wyf is mannes helpe and his confort,
> His paradys terrestre, and his disport. [E 1323 ff]

Nothing, surely, more puzzling than this confronted the dreaming poet in the Parlement, writ large in letters of black and gold over the park gate! The truth is that the issue was so fundamentally incapable of resolution, so immovably well grounded on both sides in the same ultimately unchallengeable authority, with so long and venerable a tradition to uphold either position, with Mary the perfection of womanhood and mother of grace bearing up the one, and Eve the mother of woe, source of all human ills, proving the other,—that the only thing one could do in the face of the paradox without becoming silly, was to laugh. The Fathers, seldom in the mood for laughter, had erected such a library of antifeminist diatribe as to justify the Wife's claim: "Trusteth wel, it is an impossible That any clerk wol speke good of wyves."

But a saving sense of humor had given rise to a socially satiric tradition which took the curse off the ancient grudge. One could build up one's statement of the case to such a point of extravagance /589/ that it would topple into absurdity by its own weight. But in a world more dependent on the ear for its enjoyment of literature than on the eye, it was better not to leave things to ironic implication, best to state the contrary meaning in direct assertion. Laughter followed immediately when the contradiction was inescapable to the most vagrant attention. A simple example from Balliol MS 354 will establish the pattern. The first two stanzas are as follows:

> In euery place ye may well see,
> That women be trewe as tirtyll on tree,
> Not lyberall in langage, but euer in secree,
> & gret Ioye a-monge them ys for to be.
> of all Creatures women be best:
> Cuius contrarium verum est.
> The stedfastnes of women will neuer be don,
> So Ientyll, so courtes they be euery-chon,
> Meke as a lambe, still as a stone,
> Croked nor Crabbed ffynd ye none!
> of all Creatures women be best:
> Cuius contrarium verum est.[11]

---

[11] R. H. Robbins, *Secular Lyrics of the XIVth and XVth Centuries* (1952), p. 35.

Is this the inspiration of Chantecler's perverse but discreet Latin lesson
to Madam Pertelote?

There are subtler forms. For example:

> Whan sparowys bild chirches & stepulles hie,
> & wrennes Cary Sakkes to the mylle,
> & curlews cary clothes horsis for to drye,
> & semewes bryng butter to þe market to sell,
> & woddowes were wodknyffes theves to kyll,
> & griffons to goslynges don obedyence—
> Than put in a woman your trust & confidence.[12]

Subtler still, but appealing too exclusively to the eye-reader for our present purpose, were the verses that by arranging for alternative pauses
reversed the sense of the lines at will.[13]

A more ambitious exercise in paradox was the statement of opposites
in separate poems, like the pair in the Vernon MS, and BM Add. 22283,
of which one has the refrain-line at the close of each stanza, "For hos
seiþ þe soþe, he schal be schent," and the /590/ other, "But he sey soth
he schal be schent."[14] On the analogy of songs of love and praise to the
Virgin, there are songs in general praise of Women that go to the limit
of sense and, if sincere, were bound to evoke their mocking counterparts. Such a one is the Vernon poem, "Of Women cometh this worldes
weal,"[15] to which it were "an impossible" for any clerk not to retort.
The tradition of the palinode, of course, has a very long history; and it
is hard not to suspect its permeating influence in many places where no
one would find a deliberate and formal adoption of it. What else, in
fact, is the third book of Andrew the Chaplain's *De arte honeste amandi*
but the providential antidote to the rest of the work? And what else is
the rude and heretical engraftment of Jean de Meun on Guillaume's rose-
tree but a variety of the same impulse to restore the balance? Chaucer's
own work is full of contrary strands, whereof the Clerk's palinode is but
the most notorious example.

As has been suggested, when the intention is satirical there is never
traditionally any attempt to conceal the fact in covert irony. The satire
often seems to take its rise in a kind of righteous indignation, with
irony an incidental by-product. The irony is not so much aimed for as
involuntary, and is fully and openly shared with the whole audience.
We seldom find the mask kept up throughout but rather an alternation

---

[12] *Op. cit.*, p. 103.
[13] *Op. cit.*, p. 101–02.
[14] Carleton Brown, *Religious Lyrics of the XIVth Century* (1924), pp. 152, 205.
[15] *Op. cit.*, p. 174.

between defiant assertion of what is felt to be the truth and ironic assertion of the contrary. This devil-may-care strategy is well seen in a
poem just mentioned, "Who says the sooth, he shall be shent," of which
the procedure may be outlined in abridgement:

> The man who would live easy, I count his purpose not worth a pea unless
> he devote himself to glosing the world. Flatter and pretend; let heart and
> mouth be twain; for the truth-teller shall be disgraced. The needy man shall
> find friendship faint. . . . We may curse the times when everybody bleeds
> thus inwardly. . . . Let the sycophant feed his lord with flattery and lead
> him on with lies, blind him with blandishment. He is always in dread of
> losing his place, for if he tells the truth, down he goes. And it's all wrong,
> for how can a physician heal a wound unless he probe it? But folk lie in
> wait for the unwary; and since things are thus, and going from bad to worse,
> take my advice: whoso tells the truth he shall be undone. /591/

Lydgate's poem, "Beware of Doubleness," turns the cheveril glove inside out. It begins:

> This worlde is ful of variaunce
>   In euery thing, whoo taketh hede,
> That fayth and trust and al constaunce
>   Exiled ben, this is no drede;
>   And, safe oonly in womanhede,
> I kan see no sykernesse;
>   But for al that, yet as I rede,
> Be-ware alwey of doublenesse.[16]

The other stanzas, with due mention of faithful Dalilah, Rosamond, and
Cleopatra, all likewise celebrate the truth and steadfastness of Women.
Lydgate provides a companion-piece, "Examples against Women," in
which he elaborates the falsehood and iniquity of "Dalilah the double,"
Rachel, and Judith.

One at least of these "archewyves" is already familiar to us from the
panegyric in the tale of January. The order of the procession, with Eve
at the head, is: Rebecca, Judith, Abigail, and Esther. In the same order,
with intention to show how "many a womman hath ben ful good, and
. . . hir conseils ful hoolsome and profitable," Dame Prudence had introduced them to Melibeus: Rebecca, Judith, Abigail, and Esther; ending
with the Lord's words when He gave Eve to Adam ("make we to hym
an helpe semblable to hymself") as the clinching point of the case. As
we know, Chaucer had borrowed Prudence's list from his own prose,

---

16 John Lydgate, *Minor Poems*, ed. Henry Noble MacCracken, EETS, Original Series,
No. 192 (1934), II, 438.

putting it to satirical use in his verse. It had reached him through the
French, from Albertanus' Latin—a *hortus siccus* wherein also Alice of
Bath had sometime gone a-blackberrying. It is almost symbolic, the way
Prudence, quoting proverbs about riotous women, protesting "and sire,
by youre leve, that am not I," is echoed by the Wife's "He spak to hem
that wolde lyve parfitly, And lordynges, by youre leve, that am nat I'";
and reechoed by January's "lyve in chastitee ful holily: But sires, by
youre leve, that am nat I."

It is obvious, then, how humorously ambiguous was the "climate of
opinion" in which these allusions lived in the poet's mind and memory.
Indeed, from the Melibeus also, before he is done, even Queen Proserpina gets help in rebutting Pluto's appeal to Solomon, who had found no
good woman: /592/

> He mente thus, that in sovereyn bontee
> Nis noon but God,

she repeats after Prudence, who had declared, "the entente of Salomon
was this, that as in sovereyn bountee he foond no womman; this is to
seyn, that ther is no wyght that hath sovereyn bountee save God allone."
In this *va-et-vien* of authority interchangeably invoked on either side it
is impossible to find any private violence of conviction either feminist or
anti-feminist in Chaucer himself, or any ultimate need to reach a negative
decision. The more serious he was in taking the Melibeus for his own
story, the less serious he was in the present one. Rather, he must have
seen himself as traversing, for his own and his hearers' entertainment,
well-beaten ground equally familiar to them and to him. The subject was
perennially amusing, perennially good for lively argument, hoary with
tradition and ever fresh. Who that had lived at all in the world could
imagine that there was anything really new to be said or that the debate
would ever be settled?

The panegyric on marriage at the beginning of the tale of January displays, then, the typical features of humorous anti-feministic tradition.
There is the usual cumulative exaggeration to the limits of the ridiculous,
the usual wavering line to introduce the denial of the ironic extravagance, the usual citation of illustrious examples, Janus-faced. The satire
at times grows almost boisterous in excess:

> And namely whan a man is oold and hoor . . .
> Thanne sholde he take a yong wyf and a feir . . .
> She nys nat wery hym to love and serve,
> Thogh that he lye bedrede, til he sterve . . .
> How myghte a man han any adversitee
> That hath a wyf?

> Al that hire housbonde lust, hire liketh weel;
> She seith nat ones 'nay' whan he seith 'ye.'
> 'Do this,' seith he; 'Al redy, sire,' seith she . . .
> He may nat be deceyved, as I gesse,
> So that he werke after wyves reed . . .

To such sentiments there could be but one response, and any audience, especially of Chaucer's time, could be counted on to make it. They were at home in this territory, the landmarks were familiar. It was but gilding the lily—yet also traditional—to add /593/ what Theophrastus said to the contrary, with violent mock denunciations; and then to declare in the next breath:

> But drede nat, if pleynly speke I shal,
> A wyf wol laste, and in thyn hous endure,
> Wel lenger than thee lyst, peraventure!

The *senex amans* is also, certainly, a stock butt from classical days onward, and the only wonder would be to find him treated with sympathy, not scorn. That indeed is hardly January's lot, though I think the savagery of his treatment has been magnified under the influence of a *parti pris.* January is contemptible in his blind folly, but it is only in the description of him on his wedding-night that he suddenly becomes repulsive and May at the same moment pitiable. After he is stricken with physical blindness, and especially in his acceptance of misfortune—

> For whan he wiste it may noon oother be,
> He paciently took his adversitee—

January himself goes near to becoming the object of pity. And pity is sib to sympathy, not cynicism.

The preposterousness of the denouement is sufficient notice that we are back in the cloud-cuckoo-land of the Fabliau, where sentiment is merely irrelevant—as ill-bestowed as it would be on an animated cartoon. For any one to suppose that May's self-defense could be intended or expected to be received as damning evidence of the "doublenesse" of women,—as an honest though satirical indictment—must be reckoned one of the stranger aberrations of critical judgment.

Moreover, to see the king and queen of Faerie in this story as "the dusky gods of Hades" is to misread the text in favor of a prior commitment.[17] No doubt "Chaucer knew better," as Tatlock declares,—that is, knew the classical idea of Pluto and Proserpina. The significant fact is

---

[17] Tatlock, *MP*, XXXIII, 372.

that he makes no use of it here, deliberately preferring the medieval
tradition, itself dignified with a life centuries long. Recall Campion's
delicate lute-song, a stanza of which is enough to convey the spirit of
that other tradition:

> All you that will hold watch with Love,
>   The fairy queen Proserpina
> Will make you fairer than Dione's dove. /594/

> Roses red, lilies white,
>   And the clear damask hue,
> Shall on your cheeks alight.
> Love will adorn you.[18]

Clearly, there is nothing fuliginous in the picture before us:

> Bright was the day, and blew the firmament;
> Phebus hath of gold his stremes doun ysent,
> To gladen every flour with his warmnesse.

It was June, in a garden of indescribable beauty. So passing fair was it
that the gods had chosen it for their favorite resort, and the world was
all before them where to choose:

> Ful ofte tyme he Pluto and his queene,
> Proserpina, and al hire fayerye,
> Disporten hem and maken melodye
> Aboute that welle, and daunced

under the laurel-tree ever green. They came not for deploring dumps or
to shun the light of day. (Proserpina had always loved flowers: they
provided, it might be mischievously noted, the occasion of her first
meeting her husband.) Whence did Sedgewick fetch his "little mean
dark people," his "little dark Pluto"[19]—unless perchance from Wagner?

> And so bifel, that brighte morwe-tyde,
> That in that gardyn, in the ferther syde,

Pluto, in a scene of color, light, and life, entered with Proserpina and
her numerous company of ladies-in-waiting, chose a bank fresh and
green, seated himself—and abruptly proceeded to make several entirely
unsolicited, quite unguarded, and (under the circumstances) infuriating

---

[18] E. H. Fellowes, *English Madrigal Verse* (1920), p. 593 (from Philip Rosseter, *A Booke of Ayres*, 1601, Song 19).

[19] Sedgewick, *loc. cit.*, pp. 342–3.

observations to his Queen, even calling down upon her person and all her sex wild-fire and pestilence because, forsooth, the blind old man yonder—whom Pluto calls "this honurable knyght"—is about to suffer indignities. In reproof of the man's wife "and othere mo," he declares by his high majesty that he will restore January's sight. He has really exceeded the measure; and Proserpina understandably casts courtesy aside, and /595/ gives him an inkling of what lies at her heart. Before her wrath Solomon himself is laid low:

> What make ye so much of Salomon? . . .
> Pardee, as faire as ye his name emplastre,
> He was a lecchour and an ydolastre,
> And in his elde he verray God forsook,
> And if that God ne hadde, as seith the book,
> Yspared him for his fadres sake, he sholde
> Have lost his regne rather than he wolde.

After much more of the same, "Don't be angry any longer," pleads her husband: "I give up. But I must keep my word about the man's sight." "And I mine," she replies:

> Hir answere shal she have, I undertake;

and as if to exemplify the advice that we heard at the start—

> Suffre thy wyves tonge, as Catoun bit;
> She shal comande, and thou shalt suffren it,
> And yet she wole obeye of curteisye—

she magnanimously concludes:

> Lat us namoore wordes heerof make;
> For sothe, I wol no lenger yow contrarie.   (!)

There needed no spirits from the Otherworld to bring us these illuminations! Is it too vitiated to find this farcical interlude amusing, or must we deny that its author composed it *con bravura e con gusto*? Is there no more appropriate response to such a headlong *glissade* than the sage observation of Tatlock: "The deceitful and the unfair in the feminine is indeed eternal; heaven does not redress the balance of earth"? How did *heaven* get into the act—except by way of Proserpina's breathtaking appeal to 'very God' to confirm the fact of women's truth and constancy?

The high fantasy of the wedding feast, done with such verve; the personifying sententious interjections of the narrator: "O perilous fyr— O famulier foo—O servant traytour—O Januarie, dronken in plesaunce

—O sely Damyan, allas!—O sodeyn hap! O thou Fortune unstable—O brotil joye! o sweete venym queynte!— O noble Ovyde" and the rest: these may be looked on as characterizing traits of the speaker. But such invocatory passages are scattered so plentifully through Chaucer's work that they cannot be taken as dramatically individualizing. They are formal "colours" of his own rhetorical practice, introduced only for /596/ stylistic effect, sometimes with serious intent, sometimes as here with mock solemnity, depending on the context and pervading tone.

All in all, then, if we consider the poem as an independent work written for separate reading by its author, without a dramatic frame but as another high card played in the unending Game between the Sexes, in that social frame it will not be found to stand in need of explanation or external support. Whether or not Chaucer had a pilgrim in mind to whom he might assign it, there is no intrinsic evidence that he was working at it from a point of view predetermined by such a character, as if conditioned by the events of a fictitious autobiography. And I see no reason why the poet should have expected that, taken by itself, the piece would strike its hearers as beyond the pale of traditional antifeminist japery.

But when, for reasons not now to be recaptured, he decided to give it to the Merchant, he could see, if he turned back to the General Prologue, that he had done nothing to prepare for such a story from that worthy. Hence, as Tatlock wrote many years ago, "In order to account for the feeling with which the Merchant speaks of woman and marriage, *ex post facto* domestic infelicity was manufactured for him, of which there is not a hint in the *General Prologue*." [20] The new prologue solved the immediate awkwardness by inventing adequate motivation; but what the poet may not at once have realized is that the explanation he had provided worked an instant sea-change on the story itself. The Merchant's misogyny impregnated the whole piece with a mordant venom, inflaming what originally had been created for the sake of mirth. That Chaucer could have foreseen this effect is very unlikely. There the finished piece lay; and he probably did not touch a work which had already acquired in his mind the stamp and feeling of his original purpose, reinforced perhaps by the social fixative. Whether he later became aware of what had happened might depend largely on whether he had the experience of reading the whole thing through, prologue and all, to a new audience, hearing it with their ears. Even had he done so, he might have been little struck by the novelty. And, supposing he did perceive it, he may have decided that it were best ignored. It was not the kind of problem his generation worried over.

---

[20] Tatlock, *Development and Chronology*, p. 209.

Robert M. Jordan

The Non-Dramatic Disunity
of the *Merchant's Tale**

Until very recently the *Merchant's Tale* has been the least controversial of all the Canterbury Tales. Several generations of critics have been united in scandalized astonishment over the un-Chaucerian qualities of the tale. Tatlock expressed the prevailing view in these often quoted words: "For unrelieved acidity the *Merchant's Tale* is approached nowhere in Chaucer's works. . . . Without a trace of warm-hearted tolerance or genial humor, expansive realism or even broadly smiling animalism, it is ruled by concentrated intelligence and unpitying analysis."[1] A generation earlier Kittredge had called the tale a "frenzy of contempt and hatred," and a generation later Hugh Holman brought together all the old terms, "savagely obscene, angrily embittered, pessimistic, and unsmiling," and contributed his own "dark cynicism."[2]

Now Bertrand Bronson has risen to suggest, very persuasively, I think, that the tale is much more humorous and good-natured than has been hitherto acknowledged.[3] I wish to adduce support for such an interpretation from a structural and stylistic analysis of the tale. It can be shown,

---

* Reprinted from *Publications of the Modern Language Association,* LXXVIII (September, 1963), 293–99, by permission of the author and the Modern Language Association of America. This paper was read in shortened form at the annual meeting of the MLA in Chicago, 1961.

[1] J. S. P. Tatlock, "Chaucer's *Merchant's Tale,*" *MP*, XXXIII (1936), 367.

[2] G. L. Kittredge, "Chaucer's Discussion of Marriage," *MP*, IX (1912), 435–467; C. Hugh Holman, "Courtly Love in the *Merchant's* and the *Franklin's Tales,*" *ELH*, XVIII (1951), 241–252. Both are reprinted in *Chaucer: Modern Essays in Criticism,* ed. Edward Wagenknecht (New York: Oxford Galaxy, 1959). The same view is expressed by G. G. Sedgewick, "The Structure of the *Merchant's Tale,*" *UTQ*, XVII (1948), 337–345; and Germaine Dempster, *Dramatic Irony in Chaucer* (New York: Humanities Press, 1959), pp. 46–58.

[3] Bertrand H. Bronson, "Afterthoughts on the *Merchant's Tale,*" *SP*, LVIII (October 1961), 583–596. The only other comic interpretation is John C. McGalliard, "Chaucerian Comedy: The *Merchant's Tale,* Jonson, and Molière," *PQ*, XXV (1946), 343–370.

I believe, that the tale is not the kind of organically unified characterization of a vicious and demented personality which it is conventionally assumed to be. In fact it will be seen that the demonstrable irregularity of the tale precludes the kind of intensity of concentration upon which the traditional interpretation depends. The *Merchant's Tale* is an extraordinarily *un*-unified tale, bristling with discordant elements. Once the pervasive influence of a supposedly full and rich psychological characterization of the teller is revealed not to exist, we are able to respond in a more relaxed fashion to the humor of the tale, a humor that is sometimes subtle and ironic, sometimes exuberant and coarse. We should not be dismayed to find that Chaucer did not labor to integrate and polish these diverse elements into a consistent, harmonious whole.

The fact that the humor of the tale is so rarely discussed in print may be explained by Tatlock's allusion to shame. In undertaking his study of the tale he says, "One might feel half-ashamed of so greatly enjoying so merciless a tale." For Tatlock, though, the redeeming grace is that prolonged analysis ends "in cheerfully detaching us from the prevailing mood." Since even Tatlock allows that we derive joy from the tale, we are left with two possible avenues of critical response. Either we undergo severe visitations of guilt and shame for taking pleasure in the obscene, the merciless, and the savage, or we reexamine the major premise of our interpretation, in the hope of finding that the tale is not so relentlessly bitter and destructive. The latter is of course the alternative I wish to undertake.

The "savage" interpretation evolves from the very heavy emphasis which the prologue to the tale has been forced to bear. This outcry of conjugal grief—an explosive reaction to the tale of patient Griselda—indeed compels our attention. As an impulsive and direct expression of a bitter personal disillusionment it both shocks and engrosses us. But it is a failure of discretion to read the broad-ranging and unusually diffuse *Merchant's Tale* in the narrow light of this moment of anguish. As I shall show, the disparate and often elaborately developed parts of the tale are many times totally dissonant with the attitude of bitter despair expressed in the prologue. And yet the prevailing interpretation has uncompromisingly imposed a prism of bitterness over the tale and read everything through it.[4] What does not at once *seem* savage has been too easily corrected by appeals to irony, and thus this most puzzling and inconsistent of all the Canterbury Tales has been simply and surely "unified."

---

[4] The imprudence of this procedure is pointed out by Bronson (p. 584), who reminds us that "in approximately half of the more complete MSS of the Canterbury Tales, there is no Merchant's Prologue."

The language of the prevailing commentary reveals the bias which has, in my belief, blurred the real character of the tale. Speaking of the /294/ Merchant, Sedgewick insists that "we must always remember that he is uncontrolledly angry, and therefore that the tale must always be read as sharpened into his own mood."[5] Severe distortion is bound to result when we compress into so simple a formula elements as strikingly incongruous as the various sections of the tale. A cursory view of the narrative distinguishes these four more or less clearly defined divisions: the rhetorical debate on marriage (almost one half of the entire tale, to line 1699), the courtly romance centering in the garden, the episode of Pluto and Proserpina, and the raucous fabliau episode of the conclusion. According to Tatlock and the traditional interpretation, a "concentrated intelligence and unpitying analysis" fuses all of these elements into a thoroughgoing, organic unity, expressive of the complex psyche of a cynical, embittered man. What I wish to show is that the governing intelligence is *not* concentrated, and that the psyche of the Merchant of the prologue is not a satisfactory focal point for defining a dramatic unity. Although my approach is largely negative, I have a positive purpose. I believe it is possible to be just as pleased with what *is* there as with what we think ought to be there. If we do not find an organic unity based in the character of the Merchant we need not be disappointed; there are other kinds of unity, and other kinds of satisfaction, as a fresh look at the tale will reveal.

The long encomium on marriage at the beginning of the tale has attracted much notice. Like most Chaucerian problems, it has been solved through irony. Kittredge calls it "one of the most amazing instances of sustained irony in all literature," and he sees no reason to wonder at it. The ironic over-praise of wedlock is for him a "perfect expression of the Merchant's frenzy of contempt and hatred." But if we attend more carefully to this long section of the tale we shall find, I believe, that it does not sustain the effect of dramatic irony.[6] Try as we might to maintain a sense of an embittered husband *pretending* to praise matrimony —and we must envision a remarkably poised and subtle raconteur—the illusion disintegrates after twenty or thirty lines, about one-fifth of the way through the encomium. We are indeed enmeshed in a web of irony as the speaker asks (1. 1288), "Who is so trewe, and eek so ententyf / To kepe hym, syk and hool, as is his make?" But the Merchant of the prologue has no part in the irony. The speaker before us at this point—how-

[5] "The Structure of the *Merchant's Tale*," p. 340.

[6] John M. Manly, pursuing the question of suitability of tale to teller, registered a dissent similar to mine in his note to this passage in his edition, *Chaucer's Canterbury Tales* (New York, 1928), p. 596.

ever inconsistent with dramatic propriety—is actually the familiar
Chaucerian innocent, here undertaking the glorification of marriage. Our
amusement arises from his notable lack of success. His approach is
academic, as indicated by the extended paraphrase of Theophrastus (ll.
1295–1310). He of course could not have chosen a less likely instrument
for the advancement of his stated purpose than the notorious antifeminist Theophrastus. And the only opposition he brings to bear against the
long and eloquent denunciation of women and wedlock is his petulant
question, "What force though Theofraste liste lye?" We are entertained
by the spectacle of so solemn and pedantic an orator unwittingly de-
molishing his own position. This is high comedy, not savagery.

The panegyric on marriage continues with the exempla of gentle,
loving women. Among the good wives cited are Rebecca, who to save her
son betrayed her husband, and Judith, who wrought violent death upon
Holofernes. The whole long passage is a crazy-quilt of assertions and
examples which do not quite coincide with the sentiment they purport
to advance. The humorous imbalance is sustained by the closing remarks
of the eulogizer of matrimony:

> Housbonde and wyf, what so men jape or pleye,
> Of worldly folk holden the siker weye;
> They been so knyt ther may noon harm bityde,
> And namely upon the wyves syde.   (1389-92)

There is no savage Merchant here. The irony is purely of a local kind.
It is integrally concerned with the humor of the passage and does not
extend beyond the immediate situation.

The encomium is an independent, self-contained chapter in the endless
book against women. Its humor derives from a technique frequently
practiced by Chaucer. Words and meaning stand slightly awry; appearance and truth are rendered askew. The imagination is baffled by the
effort to retain through this long and complex discourse on women and
wedlock the sense of an embittered husband speaking in a "frenzy of
contempt and hatred." Such a reading can be produced only by an
inordinate effort of the intellect and will.

There is of course a relevance between the emergent point of the
mock-encomium and the feelings of the Merchant. Both are against
women. But the relevance is loose and nominal, not organically dependent upon a thoroughgoing characterization of the Merchant. The mock-
/295/ encomium is an independently worked out satire on women which
has its own lineage in the academic anti-feminist tradition. It fits into
the *Merchant's Tale* only because the subject— women and wedlock—is
relevant, not because it sustains or develops the illusion of an embittered,

darkly cynical husband. The delicate play of viewpoints, the amusing self-defeat of the solemn moralist—these are the marks of the poet Chaucer, not of the stolid, cynical merchant-husband he has sketched in the prologue. Chaucer has freely displaced one speaker, viewpoint, and mood by another—the bitter bourgeois husband by the foolish academic debater. He has done this in total disregard of consistency of characterization and organic unity of structure and style.

Unity disintegrates at other points in the tale as well. Once the possibility of inconsistency of illusion is admitted one need only take a broad glance at the tale as a whole to see what a pastiche it is. The first half, as I have indicated, consists almost exclusively of rhetoric—long speeches, elaborately developed, whose burden is lore, the ancient and much distilled wisdom of classical and patristic commentators on women and wedlock. Prancing around and occasionally through these disquisitions is the old goat January, serving the minimum requirements of narrative continuity. But the first half of the tale, unlike the second, is almost entirely talk, with very little action or movement of any kind. The essence is rhetoric and its ironic manipulation. The second half is a courtly romance, suitably distorted and debased to accord with the anti-feminist and anti-romantic bias of the story. The important point is that although the second half is related to the first in plot and subject, the two parts are independent literary entities so far as style, tone, attitude, and general feeling are concerned. The speaker who describes the garden in the second half of the tale is a sophisticated literary man, one who is steeped in the courtly tradition:

> He [January] made a gardyn, walled al with stoon;
> So fair a gardyn woot I nowher noon.
> For, out of doute, I verraily suppose
> That he that wroot the Romance of the Rose
> Ne koude of it the beautee wel devyse;
> Ne Priapus ne myghte nat suffise,
> Though he be god of gardyns, for to telle
> The beautee of the gardyn and the welle,
> That stood under a laurer alwey grene.   (2029–37)

I think no plea of sustained dramatic irony can persuade the imagination that this speaker is identical to the foolish encomiast of the beginning of the tale, *or* to the embittered husband of the Merchant's Prologue, *or* to the single-minded business man of the General Prologue, whose "resons" were always "sownynge . . . th'encrees of his wynnyng."

To define the attitude of the tale toward the characters is another difficulty which is not satisfactorily resolved in terms of the life and temperament of the Merchant. It is generally agreed that January is the surrogate for the Merchant and the central figure of the tale. I have been urging that the correlation between the Merchant and the tale as a whole is much less consistent and thoroughgoing than has been supposed, and I would like to point out here that January is much less central to the first half of the tale than to the second. While in the latter he at least takes a prominent part in the events, in the rhetorical half of the tale January, though the instigator of the discussion, remains little more than a name put to a stock viewpoint which forms a part of the long and diffuse debate on wedlock. The imbalance between the kinds of role January plays in the two parts of the tale adds to its general disunity.

Traditionally January has been taken very seriously as a character. Even in the comic interpretation offered by Mr. McGalliard the "full and rich psychological characterization" of January is found to be the foundation and shaping purpose of the entire tale.[7] All of the elements of the tale, even the rhetorical roles of Placebo and Justinus, are taken to be integral to the characterization of January. When January is taken so seriously as a moral agent (however immoral) it becomes very difficult to see the tale as a comedy, despite Mr. McGalliard's comparisons with Molière. There is no disagreement, of course, over the kind of person January is, only about the degree to which he controls the total effect of the tale. It is difficult to find the kind of characterization which Mr. Mc-Galliard describes as "whole men" who "act and move and live in society . . . as husbands, fathers, brothers, citizens, heads of a household." Those who would see the *Merchant's Tale* as this kind of rich and unified dramatization of a "whole man" must disregard to an alarming extent the discontinuities and irrelevancies characteristic of Chaucer's narrative method. For example, the narrator's encomium on wedlock, though touched off by some rash remarks of January, can not easily be seen as part of a "full and rich psychological characterization" of January. Rather is it a lavish disquisition, superimposed upon the /296/ meager words and actions of January, serving to elucidate the anti-feminist theme of the tale. The encomium exemplifies a distinct narrative method—that of giving voice to a viewpoint extrinsic to the action—which invalidates at once any structural comparison with drama. Chaucer's method does not allow for the organic development of character through action.

Primarily Chaucer's narrative method serves to distance us from the characters. In so far as the *Merchant's Tale* is seriously concerned with January at all, it displays him as a spectacle which we witness from a safe distance. Clearly he is a gross and foolish old man, but to measure our response to him in terms of either revulsion or pity is to assume a kind of

---

[7] "Chaucerian Comedy . . . ," *PQ*, XXV (1946), p. 354.

intimacy which the structure of the narrative does not in fact allow. Mr.
Bronson has said that in the case of January and May in the denouement
sentiment is irrelevant.[8] I would add that in the tale as a whole Chaucer's
techniques of distancing support, even necessitate, such a judgment and
preclude charges of callousness or cynicism. In this tale we are involved
not with a person but with a personification. Our attention is engaged
with consequences and moral generalizations, not with personality. In
contrast to January is a character like Othello, whose situation in many
ways resembles January's. Othello is more a person and less a personification, and we are not so decisively removed from him. Engrossed with
Othello we indeed experience deeply personal and disturbing feelings.
Observing January we experience reassurances about the nature of
things. We are gratified and pleased to see that such pride and such
lechery go before precisely such a fall.

The ways in which Chaucer deploys a narrating voice define a basic
difference between narrative and drama. The many instances of the narrator's outspoken comment upon the characters and events continually
interfere with the progress of the action, and they effectively shape our
responses to the tale. Here again we shall find that charges of a "cold
intelligence" narrating with "unrelieved acidity" simply do not fit the
narrative situation. On the contrary the narrator's many and always
arresting comments show an astonishing diversity in attitude and tone.
Rather than being "unrelieved" or "cold," the mind controlling the narration is remarkably inconsistent, so much so that it cannot be com-
pressed into a unified characterization, such as that of an embittered
merchant-husband, without misrepresenting the nature of the narrative.
I have spoken of the disparity between the elegant literary tone of the
garden section and the dry academic tone of the debate section. I would
like to suggest further that the tale as a whole is an extremely varied
and discordant mixture of many of the voices which Chaucer habitually
uses. Much of the difficulty of the tale is caused by this clashing of styles,
no single one of which dominates the narration.

The voice of epic apostrophe, for example, is often heard, as at the
moment when January is struck blind. The narrator addresses Fortune
in this way:

> O sodeyn hap! o thou Fortune unstable!
> Lyk to the scorpion so deceyvable,
> That flaterest with thyn heed when thou
>   wold stynge;

---

8 "Afterthoughts . . . ," p. 593.

Thy tayl is deeth, thurgh thyn envenymynge.
O brotil joye! o sweete venym queynte!
O monstre, that so subtilly kanst peynte
Thy yiftes under hewe of stidefastnesse.
                              (2057–63)

This is the voice which, in a more leisurely narrative such as the *Man of
Law's Tale* or the *Knight's Tale*, has the scope to establish its controlling
character, although even in those tales the consistency is not as firm as
some commentators would wish. There is of course irony behind this
impassioned address to Fortune, but it does not originate in the savagery
of a disillusioned Merchant-husband.[9] The positioning of this eloquent
outcry, amid the affairs of a silly old man and his inconsequential young
wife, is a masterful piece of ironic inappropriateness. This perfectly
tempered and timed overstatement reveals not the Merchant in an un-
controlled frenzy but the poet Chaucer expressing his incomparable
sense of the ridiculous. The compassionate voice, with its moralistic over-
tones and elevated style, is the appropriate instrument for elaborating
the figure of unstable Fortune. The point of this passage is not the
sympathy expressed for January but the absurdity of expressing it in this
elevated manner. The humor depends upon our awareness that in contrast to this situation there are appropriate moments for such impassioned outcries against the order of things. The effect, once more, is
comic. The overstated concern emphasizes the true triviality of January.
The center of our interest is not January, nor is it the embittered Merchant ironically /297/pretending lamentation. Our interest centers on
the very act of elocution in which Chaucer is engaged as he launches a
beautifully eloquent—and in the context a perfectly specious and very
amusing—version of the conventional lamentation. Though January is
inconsequential as a person, and his imminent betrayal compels neither
pity nor fear, one cannot take the extreme position that January's downfall carries no moral significance whatever. The question is not whether
or not such significance exists, but how seriously it is to be taken. Very
seriously indeed, commentators have almost unanimously replied. And
accordingly the moral ramifications of January's blindness have been
diligently pursued and earnestly expounded, with the result that delight
has been vanquished by instruction.

In contrast to the overblown apostrophe to Fortune is this delightfully

---

[9] The same voice is heard in the *Nun's Priest's Tale* (ll. 3226 ff.) : "O false mordrour,
lurkynge in thy den!/O newe Scariot, newe Genylon . . ." The passage is as ironic and
humorous as that cited from the Merchant's Tale and equally irrelevant to the pilgrim-
character presumably being dramatized.

understated expression of sympathy for May as she awaits January's pleasure:

> He was al coltissh, ful of ragerye,
> And ful of jargon as a flekked pye.
> The slakke skyn aboute his nekke shaketh,
> Whil that he sang, so chaunteth he and craketh.
> But God woot what that May thoughte in hir herte,
> Whan she hym saugh up sittynge in his sherte,
> In his nyght-cappe, and with his nekke lene;
> She preyseth nat his pleyying worth a bene.
>
> (1847–54)

Again the governing viewpoint is characteristically Chaucerian in its combination of detachment and compassion (neither quality, of course, is appropriate to the Merchant). The humor of this passage, like that of the other, comes from the zest for detail and the unerring sense of contrast and timing. Here, however, our laughter comes suddenly, with the deft, playful, and masterfully abbreviated allusion to May's point of view. Our amusement is increased by the inadequacy of her response: the paraphrase of her reaction, "She preyseth nat his pleyying worth a bene," bespeaks a young lady of little sensibility and less sense, hardly a person deserving of very deep sympathy. The view that she is a "deep one," whose depths Chaucer purposely leaves to our imaginations, seems to me as unsupportable as the "psychological" interpretation of January. It originates similarly in a confusion between the critic's understanding of people and his understanding of art.

These two passages—one expressing sympathy for May, the other expressing sympathy for January—point to the crux of the critical problem. In order to achieve a consistent case for a bitter, anti-feminist speaker critics have had to undertake an extensive program of resolving contradictions. Thus the sympathetic attitude toward January is supposed to indicate the Merchant's empathy with the hero of his tale, while the derisive attitude toward January is supposed to indicate either the Merchant's disgust with himself or his blindness to the similarity to his own case. All of these are arbitrary lines of interpretation, and all are pursued on the assumption that there *is* a consistency which must be revealed. The case of May-interpretation is the same: the critic feels compelled to shape contradictions into a unitary hypothesis. These multiple appeals to irony result in an enlargement of the Merchant's sensibilities far beyond the meager indications provided by the text. Ultimately the critic following such roads can say only that the tale expresses the infinite possibilities of the human psyche. When we reach this point criticism is lost and art is

robbed of all meaning. It is much more fruitful—although it may sound
banal in the age of New Criticism and scientific method—to examine the
work dispassionately and without preconceptions, with an aim to define
its unique character.

In an original approach to the tale C. A. Owen, Jr., has enlarged upon
the dramatic interpretation and found that "the controlling images in
the poem . . . are the linked ones of the garden, the blindness, and the
tree."[10] For Mr. Owen the tale is a unified matrix of images. Thus one
"crucial passage" early in the tale, which begins "Mariage is a ful greet
sacrament," is found to send "echoes and reverberations through the two
consultations and the marriage to a crowning climax in the garden scene
at the end." The first difficulty with this approach is that one passage
is no more crucial than any other. One can drop his finger at random
anywhere in the text and find something about marriage, and any of the
foolishness in the tale (of which there is much) can be interpreted as
"blindness." The debatable question is the mode and character of the
relationship in which such passages exist. Mr. Owen reads the tale as
the unified symbolic enlargement of an idea present in January's mind
from the beginning. In doing so he disregards both the irregular structure of the narrative and the humor. He maintains that "the story does
not stop with a single literal fulfillment. Through Proserpina's vow it
suggests repetition through the ages. And it creates in the literal world
the /298/ symbolic fulfillment of the idea." Reverberating symbolism
of this kind may be characteristic of Shakespearean tragedy, but such a
reading seems to me quite out of phase with the discontinuities and the
humor of the *Merchant's Tale*. The ingenious unification belongs more
to the critic than to the tale. It culminates in an enforcement of the
moral lesson, along the lines of the traditional interpretation of the tale:
"The Merchant participates in the blindness of his creature January in
not realizing the extent to which he is talking of his own sore in the
tale." Malvolio's virtue has once more triumphed over Chaucer's cakes
and ale.

The difficulties I have been considering have led some critics to suggest that the tale was not originally intended for the Merchant. A. C.
Baugh, for example, cited textual evidence, such as the line "As doon
thise fooles that been seculeer," to argue assignment to an ecclesiastic,
and the Friar seemed the most likely.[11] Retaliation was quick, in the
name of intensity, coherence, and irony, all of which qualities depend

---

10 "The Crucial Passages in Five of *The Canterbury Tales*: A Study in Irony and
Symbol," *JEGP*, LII (1953), 299. Reprinted in *Chaucer: Modern Essays in Criticism*.

11 "The Original Teller of the *Merchant's Tale*," *MP*, XXXV (1937), 15–26. Manly
(*C.T.*, p. 624) suggests the Monk.

upon preserving the character of a bitter Merchant-narrator.[12] My own argument, nihilistic though it may seem, is that it makes no difference which pilgrim one wishes to assign to the tale. None will fit, for the tale does not "characterize" a single, unified pilgrim-personality. The basis of Chaucer's art is not the so-called dramatic principle, but rather an aesthetic principle which we are just beginning to understand.

The fairy section is more damaging to a unitary hypothesis than any of the elements so far considered. This episode illustrates very well what Charles Muscatine has pointed out as the Gothic tendency of Chaucer's art to follow the principle of juxtaposition of parts, as distinguished from continuous development of one part into an organic whole.[13] The squabble between Pluto and Proserpina is a self-contained episode (ll. 2219–2319) of delightfully humorous character. Its presence in the tale is justified by the relevance of its subject matter; but while we can say that it fits into the tale, we cannot say that it develops the characterization of the Merchant. In fact it bears a very strong negative relation to our sense of either an embittered husband or a purposeful business man. The tone and style are highly cultivated:

> Bright was the day, and blew the firmament....
> And so bifel, that brighte morwe-tyde,
> That in that gardyn, in the ferther syde,
> Pluto, that is kyng of Fayerye,
> And many a lady in his compaignye,
> Folwynge his wyf, the queene Proserpyna,
> Which that he ravysshed out of Ethna
> Whil that she gadered floures in the mede—
> In Claudyan ye may the stories rede,
> How in his grisely carte he hire fette—
> This kyng of Fairye thanne adoun hym sette
> Upon a bench of turves, fressh and grene ...
> (2219, 2225–35)

Like the earlier debate carried on by January and his advisers, the contest between Pluto and his wife derives its materials from the antifeminist tradition. A minimal relevance to the tale as a whole is thereby assured, despite the structural imbalance and stylistic incongruity. The dramatic vitality of the scene, reminiscent of the *Nun's Priest's Tale*, readily engages our interest at the same time that it must dismay the

---

[12] Germaine Dempster, "The Original Teller of the *Merchant's Tale*," *MP*, XXXVI (1938), 1–8.

[13] *Chaucer and the French Tradition* (Berkeley and Los Angeles, Calif., 1957), pp. 167–173.

reader intent upon continuity and consistency. Despite the fact that Proserpina has the last word, the eternal wiliness of the female has been fully displayed in the process. The emergent viewpoint of the episode is masculine, and this is what makes the rendering of Proserpina's victory so amusing—even for a female reader, I should think. But as in the earlier marriage debate, there is no justification for identifying the general anti-feminist viewpoint with the specific cynicism of the Merchant. The fairy episode is another self-contained element which fulfills its own character before it contributes to the structure of the tale as a whole.

The lively finale of the tale offers further difficulties for those who would insist upon consistency, and further entertainment for the less demanding. The act of betrayal in the pear tree is narrated in a manner quite outside the character of a merciless Merchant; January stoops down,

> and on his bak she stood,
> And caughte hire by a twiste, and up she gooth—
> Ladyes, I prey you that ye be nat wrooth;
> I kan nat glose, I am a rude man—
> And sodeynly anon this Damyan
> Gan pullen up the smok, and in he throng.
>
> (2348–53)

By shattering the fictional illusion at this most untimely moment, in order to address his listeners and apologize for himself, the speaker draws attention to his own presence. It is not a presence to repel us by its frenzied expression of contempt and hatred. Far from savage, the speaker is gauche and obsequious. The posture is /299/ familiar. It is that adopted by Chaucer in the General Prologue as he apologizes that his wit is short, and in the Miller's Prologue as he dissociates himself from the churl's tale, and in many other instances in the Tales and elsewhere. The affectation of helplessness in the face of facts is part of the repertoire of the Chaucerian narrator.[14] It has nothing to do with characterization of individual pilgrims, and it is just as entertaining in the *Merchant's Tale* as elsewhere. The humor increases as this "rude man" a few moments later narrates the action attendant upon January's recovery of his sight:

> on his wyf his thoght was evermo.
> Up to the tree he caste his eyen two,
> And saugh that Damyan his wyf had dressed

---

[14] Ernst Curtius cites "affected modesty" as one of the established *topoi* of antique rhetoric sustained through the Middle Ages. *European Literature and the Latin Middle Ages,* trans. W. R. Trask (London, 1953), pp. 83–85.

In swich manere it may nat been expressed,
But if I wolde speke uncurteisly . . .
                    (2359–63)

The delicacy and solicitousness of the speaker is so obviously an affectation, in the light of the rude forthrightness he has just apologized for,
that it becomes impossible for us to look with solemnity upon the events
he is narrating. Such breaks in the narration provide a level of entertainment outside the events of the tale. The ending, taking into account
these posturings of the speaker—which, after all, *are* part of Chaucer's
art—is magnificently funny, especially if we can release ourselves from
the need to read it as part of a large-scale characterization of a darkly
cynical Merchant-narrator.

Structural and stylistic evidence seems to indicate conclusively that
there is no single viewpoint governing the narrative. The tale is less a
unified presentation than a composite of several narrating attitudes and
positions, often mutually contradictory. Each is assumed by the poet in
accordance with the demands of the particular situation. I think it is a
mistake to decry or to obscure the discontinuities that result. If there is
no "organic unity" in terms of the character of the Merchant, we should
be satisfied with the "mechanic unity" which could compose so many
comic attitudes toward lust and marriage into so diverting a tale. Ad-
mittedly the total design lacks the balance and the carefully adjusted
intricacy of the *Knight's Tale*. It also lacks the dynamism and economy
of the *Miller's Tale*. But for variety of comic approaches to folly it is
matchless. Chaucer has allowed himself an unusual amount of freedom
to improvise around the thin but firm and fertile plot of the *senex
amans*. However diffuse the tale becomes and however out of balance its
parts are with one another, a loose, composite form of unity is maintained. Although the narrative viewpoint is altogether inconsistent, the
moral viewpoint remains firm. It is revealed through the poet's exploi-
tation of the comic possibilities inherent in impropriety and incongruity.

Mortimer J. Donovan

The Image of Pluto and Proserpine in the *Merchant's Tale**

Chaucer's models for January and May of the *Merchant's Tale* appear to have been identified only in part in the literature of the feeble lover married to a much younger, totally unappreciative wife.[1] According to studies by Professors Lowes, Brown, and McGalliard, which show structural and phrasal similarities between the first part of this tale and Deschamps' *Miroir de Mariage*, January is counselled before marriage much as Franc Vouloir is, yet, unlike Franc Vouloir, is already, in fact, an old man.[2] Agapes' husband in Boccaccio's *Ameto*, as J. S. P. Tatlock pointed out, is close to January in physical features, general unattractiveness as well as age, but there the points of resemblance end.[3] Another really ancient "lover" of Chaucer's reading—Pluto himself— remains to be mentioned. In his analysis of the Pear-tree Story, Tatlock called Pluto January's "divine counterpart," but only because of his sponsorship of January's cause when May deceives her blind husband.[4] Neither Tatlock nor others, so far as I know, saw anything of Pluto and Proserpine, respectively, in the passages leading up to the Pear-tree Story. Chaucer, this study will attempt to show, may have these deities

---

* Reprinted from *Philological Quarterly*, XXXVI (January, 1957), 49–60, by permission of the author and The University of Iowa.

[1] F. N. Robinson, ed. *The Complete Works of Geoffrey Chaucer* (Boston and New York, 1933), p. 817; quotations are taken from this text. For more references to the aged lover in literature, see George R. Coffman, "Old Age from Horace to Chaucer. Some Literary Affinities and Adventures of an Idea," *Speculum*, IX (1934), 247–277.

[2] John Livingston Lowes, "Chaucer and the Miroir de Mariage," *MP*, VIII (1910–11), 165–186; Carleton Brown, "The Evolution of the Canterbury 'Marriage Groups,'" *PMLA*, XLVIII (1933), 1041–59; John C. McGalliard, "Chaucer's *Merchant's Tale* and Deschamps' *Miroir de Mariage*," *PQ*, XXV (1946), 193–220. See also W. F. Bryan and Germaine Dempster, edd. *Sources and Analogues of Chaucer's Canterbury Tales* (Chicago, 1941), pp. 333–339.

[3] J. S. P. Tatlock, "Boccaccio and the Plan of Chaucer's *Canterbury Tales*," *Anglia*, XXXVII (1913), 96–106; *S & A*, pp. 339–340.

[4] J. S. P. Tatlock, "Chaucer's *Merchant's Tale*," *MP*, XXXIII (1935–36), 372; *S & A*, pp. 341 ff.

94

in mind from the start as he individualizes his aged lover and young wife.

In the course of the *Merchant's Tale* Chaucer mentions by title a poem in which these deities appear, Claudian's *De Raptu Proserpinae:* /50/

> Pluto that is kyng of Fayerye,
> And many a lady in his compaignye,
> Folwynge his wyf, the queen Proserpyna,
> Which that he ravysshed out of Ethna
> Whil that she gadered floures in the mede—
> *In Claudyan ye may the stories rede,*
> *How in his grisely carte he hire fette.* (IV/E/2227–33)

The most significant fact which this quotation reveals is that Chaucer writes as one who knows Pluto and Proserpine so well that, in an effortless aside, he can cite a helpful reference for any reader slow to recognize the deities who sympathize with January and May, respectively, during the first *adversitee* after their marriage. Since, therefore, Chaucer's prior reading is reasonably certain, we might examine the first part of the *Merchant's Tale* and the *De Raptu* for general similarities in the characters and the situations presented; although the two poems differ radically, these similarities, because general, stand apart from the genre in which each poet consciously wrote.[5]

I

In the two poems, the lover as he is first presented illustrates what Professor Patch gives as January's dominant characteristic: "desire in old age."[6] He is lonely, unwed, childless, but so old that he has no reasonable prospect of offspring:

> Dux Erebi quondam tumidas exarsit in iras
> proelia moturus superis, *quod solus egeret*

---

[5] On Chaucer's use of Claudian, see Thomas R. Lounsbury, *Studies in Chaucer* (New York, 1892), II, 254–258. Lounsbury wrote: "There are, perhaps, not many passages which can be traced directly to this poet. There is, more often, a general resemblance in the ideas and spirit than in the transference of the lines"; see also Edgar Finley Shannon, *Chaucer and the Roman Poets*, Harvard Studies in Comparative Literature VII (Cambridge, 1929), pp. 356–358. In a recent study of Claudian's place in Chaucer's reading, Professor Robert A. Pratt demonstrated clearly the need for seeing Claudian "as Chaucer did," through a medieval text like the *Liber Catonianus:* "Chaucer's Claudian," *Speculum*, XXII (1947), 419. My present recourse to the Teubner *De Raptu* (ed. Julius Koch, Leipsig, 1893) is consistent with my purpose to treat only general parallels, some of which appear in such other texts as the *Metamorphoses*, V, 346 ff.

[6] Howard Rollin Patch, *On Rereading Chaucer* (Cambridge, 1939), p. 228.

> *conubiis sterilesque diu consumeret annos*
> *impatiens nescire torum nullasque mariti*
> *inlecebras nec dulce patris cognoscere nomen.* (ɪ, 32–36)

> To take a wyf it is a glorious thyng,
> And namely whan a man is oold and hoor;
> Thanne is a wyf the fruyt of his tresor.
> Thanne sholde he take a yong wyf and a feir,
> On which he myghte engendren hym an heir,
> And lede his lyf in joye and in solas. (ɪᴠ/ᴇ/1268–73)

From his office as possessor of the dead as well as from his age, /51/ Pluto is most unsuited to a wife as young as his niece Proserpine; at sixty years, January, who is properly named, represents a lover whose fertile years have passed. Yet each lover desires marriage for the same reasons: (1) offspring, and (2) solace. Remarkably, each has two brothers also.[7] Pluto's are Neptune, already married to Amphitrite, and Jupiter, married to Juno; January's are Justinus, who is definitely married (IV/E/ 1545), and Placebo, who at least speaks with authority on the subject of marriage.

When the two lovers lay plans for marriage, each receives help from but *one* of his two brothers. Although Neptune has little or nothing to do with Pluto's conquest of Proserpine, Jupiter, at Pluto's insistence, is an active intermediary. When Mercury carries Pluto's plea for a wife to him, Jupiter receives it in amazement: he can remember no eligible maiden who will exchange the light of day for the darkness of the Underworld (ɪ, 117–121). He then confers with Venus and decides that with her help he can remove Proserpine from the protected palace of her mother Ceres to the flowery fields of Henna, where her abduction by Pluto will be simplified. In January's deliberations, Justinus, who calls marriage *no childes pley* (IV/E/1530), is powerless before the whim of a brother who is as testy as Pluto (*tumidas exarsit in iras*) ; for Justinus' sweet reasoning and arguments, January has little respect: "Straw for thy Senek, and for thy proverbes" (IV/E/1567). Far more conciliatory, yet as doubtful as Jupiter, Placebo admits that "it is an heigh corage/Of any man that stapen is in age/To take a yong wyf" (IV/E/1513–15) ; yet, put to a categorical answer, he does not hesitate to please, whatever the cost: "I seye it is a cursed man . . . /That letteth matrimoigne, sikerly" (IV/E/1572–73). Since January finds it easy to accept this wisdom, preparations for his marriage proceed.

---

[7] Tatlock, "Chaucer's *Merchant's Tale*," p. 371, interprets Placebo and Justinus as January's "two friends." I see no reason why Chaucer's *bretheren* should not be construed as brothers in the flesh:
> Ther fil a stryf bitwixe *his* bretheren two,
> Of whiche that oon was cleped Placebo,
> Justinus soothly called was that oother (IV/E/1475–77)

In each poem, the bridge, young and in every way attractive, contrasts with her aged lover. Claudian says that Proserpine is maidenly, modest, but already old enough to be courted by Mars and Phoebus (I, 133–137); May, who is appropriately named, has a reputation for her youthful beauty: when Chaucer appraises it, /52/ he says—we shall find, prophetically: "Hire to biholde it semed *fayerye*" (IV/E/1743). Proserpine and May alike suggest fertility, new life, hope; Pluto and January suggest age, decay and death. Yet, as hopeless as Pluto and January appear, still they feel the effects of love similarly. When Jupiter views the prospects of Pluto's impending marriage, he is happy to find that love's arrow will soften the iron-clad heart of that king (I, 227–228). Like Pluto, January feels love even before he has discovered who his mate will be. His softening-up takes the form of *curious bisynesse*, dreamings at night, during which he envisions the physical type closest to his heart and, with this ideal to guide him, selects from the maidens of his town the one most pleasing to him. If Pluto's lust (II, 271) motivates the rape of Proserpine, it is lust also that prompts January's conquest of May. Of January, Chaucer says, "Were it for hoolynesse or for dotage,/I kan nat seye, but swich a greet corage/Hadde this knyght to been a wedded man" (IV/E/1253–55); but later Chaucer unequivocally describes him as "dronken in pleasaunce/In mariage" (IV/E/1788–89); like Pluto, January is to "be wedded hastily" (IV/E/1411) and shows little patience in the face of obstacles. If his victim differs from Proserpine in entering the marriage negotiations voluntarily—she makes sure that she is "feffed in" her knight's lands before she goes to church (IV/E/1698)—still her display of affection after marriage is so forced as to make her appear the object of a *raptus* as real as Proserpine's.

Even after Chaucer christianizes the union of January and May, the details of the marriage feast and the first night in the two poems are similar. Joy at last pervades the Underworld as Pluto brings his bride home; his guests dismissed, January at the close of his wedding day finds a similar joy. But more striking, though still conventional details, are the following:

> Men drynken, *and the travers drawe anon.*
> The bryde was broght abedde as stille as stoon;
> And *whan the bed was with the preest yblessed,*
> Out of the chambre hath every wight hym dressed;
> And Januarie hath faste in armes take
> His fresshe May, his paradys, his make (IV/E/1817–22).

Claudian says that Pluto's slaves close back the curtains: "alii praetexere ramis (II, 320); that Night blesses the union: "stat pronuba iuxta/ stellentes Nox picta sinus tangensque cubile/ omina perpetuo genitalia foedere sanctit" (II, 362–364). If these details /53/ are duplicated in

other prothalamia, certain others may be telling. In both poems the
bride is far from happy and is no willing partner to her husband's inept
playfulness. Chaucer is more explicit than Claudian:

> But God woot what that May thoughte in hir herte,
> Whan she hym saugh up sittynge in his sherte,
> In his nyght-cappe, an with his nekke lene;
> She preyseth nat his pleyyng worth a bene. (IV/E/1851–54)

May is so unhappy, in fact, that not long after the marriage ceremony, a
matter of a couple of days, she turns her eyes to the younger Damyan for
solace. Claudian does not say how long it is before Proserpine, after an
expected disappointment in marriage, seeks relief from Pluto, old, hoary
and lacking in every desirable quality. But she takes care to appear to
her mother in a dream and from the Underworld urges her rescue:

> quodsi non omnem pepulisti pectore matrem,
> si tua nata, Ceres, et non me Caspia tigris
> edidit, his, oro, miseram defende cavernis
> inque superna refer. prohibent si fata reverti
> vel tantum visura veni.   (III, 104–108)

Either Ceres should help Proserpine regain the Upper World or, failing
that, should visit her below: Such is her plea.

Claudian, who never finished the *De Raptu Proserpinae*, leaves off
before Jupiter, at Ceres' insistence, grants the first alternative. We know
from other sources, which were available to Chaucer also, that Proserpine is allowed to spend certain months of the year in the Upper World,
safely above the home of the dead, but just where is not clear. Her
months of freedom, in fact, coincide with the period during which plants
on earth grow, bear fruit, and prosper. Now if Chaucer, in writing the
first part of his *Merchant's Tale*, had the unfinished *De Raptu* in mind
as a source of materials for the character of both January and May, as an
examination of the two texts suggests, we may safely imagine that, even
with his source unfinished, he continued to use his epic materials in the
second part of his tale—the Pear-tree Story. In testing this assumption, we
may expect to find, first, the image of Pluto and a successfully liberated
Proserpine living out their marriage, each in character unchanged from
the deity whom Claudian has sketched, and, second, a January and May
who show marked affinities to their respective divine counterparts. /54/

II

In the Pear-tree Story itself (IV/E/2009–418), where few parallels
with the *De Raptu* are to be noted, Chaucer's selection of Pluto and

Proserpine as the divinities who look after January and May respectively is the more remarkable because here he does specify a source, if
not the very source which he consulted:

> Pluto, that is kyng of Fayerye,
> And many a lady in his compaignye,
> Folwynge his wyf, the queene Proserpyna,
> Which that he ravysshed out of Ethna
> Whil that she gadered floures in the mede—
> In Claudyan ye may the stories rede. (IV/E/2227–32)

As has been done before, the easier course is to take literally Chaucer's
casual helpfulness and to assume that his concept of the king and queen
of *fayerye* may develop from what he read in Claudian. Without noting
the similarities pointed out above between the *De Raptu* and the first
part of the *Merchant's Tale*, Theodore Spenser remarked as an "idle
assumption" that "since Claudian speaks far more than anyone else
about Pluto as hell's king . . . Chaucer had the *De Raptu* in mind when
writing these passages [i.e., the Pear-tree Story]."[8] Neglecting the *De
Raptu* altogether, Laura Hibbard Loomis cited evidence to show that
Chaucer had consulted the Middle English *Sir Orfeo*, the only writing
before the *Canterbury Tales* in which Pluto, though unnamed, passes
as king of *fayerye* and Proserpine as queen; similarities between
Chaucer and *Sir Orfeo*, however, are limited to the representation of
Pluto as a man of *trouthe* and king of the fairies.[9] In view of this disagreement, it may be safe to look further into the myth of Proserpine
as related by Claudian and explained after his time to see what it meant
to Chaucer when he wrote the Pear-tree Story. /55/

First, Chaucer places Pluto and Proserpine in January's garden, which
surpasses in beauty the garden in the *Romance of the Rose* (IV/E/2031–
33). As D. W. Robertson, Jr., found, this is but one of a series of

---

[8] "Chaucer's Hell: A Study in Mediaeval Convention," *Speculum*, II (1927), 183, n.
7. But see also OF. *Eneas*, ed. Jacques Salverda de Grave, Bibliotheca Normannica IV
(Halle, 1891):

> La jus descendent tuit li mort,
> *l'empire tient Pluto par sort,*
> *il ne est reis, et Proserpine*
> en est deessë et reïne. (Vs. 2379–82)

[9] "Chaucer and the Breton Lays of the Auchinleck MS," *SP*, XXXVIII (1941), 29:
"For this curious linking used with precisely the same artless naiveté that characterizes
the lay [*Sir Orfeo*], there appears to be no parallel save in the *Merchant's Tale*.
Chaucer, who knew all about Pluto, likewise transforms him in this one instance, name
and all, into a moralizing fairy king. He uses the concept ironically, wittily, but to
assume that this precise and most singular parallel was achieved without reference to
Orfeo is to stretch credulity too far."

medieval gardens, all more or less alike in luxuriance, beauty and detail:
the tree, the *welle* and visitors bent on pleasure.[10] In the *Merchant's
Tale,* the garden has been found to represent symbolically the sensual
beauty and occasion for *delit* which January accepts as his *hevene in
erthe*: by this time he has answered the question of heaven here or
hereafter in favor of a heaven here amid all the sensual pleasures the
world can offer; he is certain after this decision into which he talks himself (IV/E/1637–47) that a *paradys terrestre,* in his practical thinking,
is far more real than any other kind. But Chaucer, in picturing this
paradise, is faced with the necessity of making the garden look not only
pagan but also "Classical." While any reader familiar with the world-
liness ironically implied in a *verray paradys,* with *welles* or *ryveres* and
all the other trappings, would know how to accept January's garden, he
would at the same time find it a suitable setting for the Roman deities
Pluto and Proserpine. January's garden, in fact, appears close to what
Chaucer much earlier in his career considered Parnassus, the traditional
home of the gods, to be:

> Be favorable eke, thou Polymya,
> On Parnaso that with thy sustres glade,
> By Elycon, not fer from Cirrea,
> Singest with vois memorial in the shade,
> Under the laurer which that may not fade,
> And do that I my ship to haven wynne. (Vs. 15–20)

As in the *House of Fame* (v. 522), Chaucer here in *Anelida and Arcite*
makes of Helicon a *welle,* near which a laurel grows;[11] in his description
of January's garden he has Pluto and Proserpine amuse themselves, sing
and dance around the "welle,/That stood under a laurer alwey grene"
(IV/E/2036–37). Although the combination of garden, well and laurel
may appear as a commonplace, still the association of these with Classical deities in a second instance in Chaucer, *the only other in which they
appear together /56/ in his poetry,* seems to show that, in the *Merchant's
Tale,* written long after *Anelida and Arcite* (Robinson, p. 355), he is
recalling his earlier impression of Parnassus and is now describing a
pagan paradise quite literally.

---

[10] D. W. Robertson, Jr., "The Doctrine of Charity in Mediaeval Literary Gardens:
A Topical Approach through Symbolism and Allegory," *Speculum,* XXVI (1951),
44–45. See also Howard Rollin Patch, *The Other World According to Descriptions in
Medieval Literature,* Smith College Studies in Modern Languages, N. S. No. 1 (Cambridge, 1950), pp. 134–174.

[11] For a discussion of the passages in Chaucer and elsewhere in which Helicon
is so named, see Professor Root's note to *Troilus,* III, 1807–10, in *The Book of
Troilus and Criseyde* (Princeton, 1945), pp. 495–496.

This picture of Parnassus differs radically from that of Pluto's regular home, the "dirke regioun/Under the ground," which he mentions in the *Franklin's Tale* (V/F/1074–75); or of Elysium, which, according to Claudian (II, 282–285), is lighted, not by Phoebus, as in the *Merchant's Tale*, but by Pluto's private sun. In fact, January and May are very much alive and above ground as they enjoy the earthly paradise which Chaucer represents: "Bright was the day, and blew the firmament;/ *Phoebus* hath of gold his stremes doun ysent,/To gladen every flour with his warmnesse" (IV/E/2219–21). Now, if Chaucer knew, as is certain, that the married life of Proserpine, according to Jupiter's decree, is confined to two places, the unhappy Underworld and, during the fertile months of the year, the regions above; and if Pluto and Proserpine are represented in the Pear-tree Story as definitely not in the Underworld, the conclusion follows that he is placing them in the region lighted by Phoebus, in the home proper to all deities—Parnassus. Chaucer could have known the scant facts of Jupiter's decision to allow Proserpine life above the Underworld from a number of sources—the *Metamorphoses* v, 565–567, or Ovid's *Fasti*, IV, 612–14; even as a reader of Claudian's *De Raptu Proserpinae*, which he mentions in the *Merchant's Tale*, he must have been tempted to visualize Jupiter's decision as in fact realized, as any other reader of an unfinished story would. But, finding little in the above Classical accounts of Proserpine's life above earth or in later literature, he indiscriminately associates her as well as Pluto, as do the *Orfeo* poet and others, with the fairies, in accordance with what must be for him no new tradition.[12] Like such Roman /57/ deities as Pluto and Proserpine, fairies in the fourteenth century, as the Wife of Bath indicates (III/D/857–872), are not to be believed in as such and so are used by Chaucer only in a kind of fable; "Omnes dii gentium

---

[12] Mrs. Loomis, p. 29, wrote that Chaucer, in order to associate Pluto with the fairies, had to know *Sir Orfeo*, in which a Pluto-like figure is, in fact, the king of the fairies. My explanation offered here makes a simpler assumption: the widespread knowledge of the Proserpine myth as explained by Claudian and developed by later writers. When Chaucer makes of Pluto and Proserpine characters whom he calls fairies, he gives no clear evidence of associating them with any one mythology, Celtic or otherwise. *Kyng of Fairye* is a convenient term for him to describe Pluto in this phase of his life cycle, i.e., above the Underworld: as such, Pluto would be a *fée*. According to A. Hatzfeld and A. Darmesteter, *Dictionnaire Général* (Paris, 1920), *fée*, derived from the popular Latin **fata* (Classical *fatua*) means any "divinité champêtre." If Chaucer intends no more, Pluto is well described in few words: he "adoun hym sette/ Upon a bench of turves, fressh and *grene*" (IV/E/2234–35). Dunbar also sees Pluto as a divinity of the field: "There was Pluto, the elrich incubus,/In cloke of *grene*, His court usit no sable": *Poems*, ed. W. Mackay Mackenzie (Edinburgh, 1932), vs. 125–126. Elsewhere in the *Canterbury Tales* Chaucer discriminates little between Germanic and non-Germanic traditions and, in fact, uses *fairy* and *elf* (OE. *aelf*) interchangeably: "This maketh that ther been no fayeryes./For ther as wont to walken was an elf,/Ther walketh now the lymytour hymself" (III/D/872-874).

daemonia; Dominus autem caelos fecit." For purposes of Chaucer's fable, they present an advantage, for, though unseen, they can mingle with mortals, as Pluto and Proserpine do in the Pear-tree Story.

Pluto and Proserpine, however, do more than sing, dance and circulate among the seekers after refreshment in January's garden. When Pluto restores January's sight, which has been lost through "misfortune" (IV/E/2057–68; 2355), he is the familiar instrument of Fortune known to Chaucer also through the *De Consolatione Philosophiae* (III, Met. 12). But, when Proserpine retaliates by giving May a *suffisant answere* upon January's untimely discovery of his wife in Damyan's arms, Proserpine is revealing a power implied in most accounts familiar to Chaucer, and specified in Claudian's *De Raptu*, where as Pluto's queen and unwilling bride, she shares his authority, even to the point of judging the wicked, to include the self-righteous January, and rescuing the innocent, among whom she counts without reservations the ill-starred May:

> tu damnatura nocentes,
> tu requiem latura piis; te iudice sontes
> improba cogentur vitae commissa fateri. (II, 302–304)

In this role Proserpine receives from Pluto as her handmaidens the Parcae or Fates—"accipe Lethaeo famulas cum gurgite Parcas,/sitque ratum quodcumque voles" (II, 305–306) ; these in Chaucer multiply from three to "many a lady in his compaignye,/Folwynge his wyf, the queene Proserpyna" (IV/E/2228–29). If in authority she is her husband's equal, she may well stand up to Pluto in the debate to settle the matter of women's *tresons* (IV/E/2237–319). She not only succeeds as a debater, but even vanquishes Pluto, who is forced to seek mercy: " 'Dame,' quod this Pluto, 'be no lenger wrooth;/I yeve it up' " (IV/E/2311–12).

In the *Merchant's Tale*, when a thoroughly humanized Pluto /58/ and Proserpine take sides and do their utmost to help January and May respectively, they do only what might be expected of two deities, after whom Chaucer seems to have modeled his ancient knight and young lady from the start. They are like January and May not only in age, sympathy, but also in degree of cunning. Pluto, called in Claudian the harbinger of Death or Death himself (III, 237–238), is anxious to help January, who jealously protects May against unseen ravishers like Damyan; unhappy Proserpine is anxious to help unhappy May, who wants to avoid January's protection and seek love elsewhere. As Pluto stands for decay and death, so the Proserpine of Claudian stands like May for new life. Once above the Underworld, she is queen of the harvest with its fruit: "fulvis semper ditabere pomis" (II, 293). As daughter of Ceres, who herself gave mankind corn for food in accordance with Jupiter's prophecy as recorded by Claudian (III, 18–66), Proserpine shares this reputation for fecundity, which Chaucer could have known, not only from reading Claudian, but also from such other sources as St. Augustine, whom he mentions elsewhere.[13] We can say that, as her equally fruitful, equally unhappy sister, Proserpine does what is expected for May after January has discovered her with Damyan in the pear tree: just as she uses her cunning to bring about Jupiter's decree which enables her to escape from the Underworld during certain months of the year, so too she gives May the *suffisant answer* by which May escapes unharmed from January's justified anger. That Chaucer is thinking about /59/ Proserpine-like fecundity even to the end of the tale is admirably shown in aged January's final gesture toward May, when, ironically, he "on hire wombe . . . stroketh hire ful softe" (IV/E/2414).

To summarize, these parallels with the *De Raptu Proserpinae* are the more remarkable because Chaucer names Claudian's unfinished epic before going very far in the Pear-tree Story. Yet, even without this mention of a title, they could not be dismissed as accidental: almost all of them are general, but they go well together and without exception fit the narrative order of the tale perfectly. Among the points suggesting that Chaucer had the *De Raptu* in mind throughout his tale is the character of January—old, lustful, unmarried, yet craving the comforts of marriage as well as offspring. Like Pluto he has two brothers, one of whom willingly helps him to gain a bride. Although she is far less fully delineated than Proserpine, she is at least young, ready for marriage, but not to a husband whose life is about spent. When she marries, she reveals no love at all for her knight and husband: Chaucer insists that,

---

[13] In the *De Civitate Dei* (*P. L.*, XLI, col. 210) St. Augustine cites Varro's remarks: "Et hanc ipsam [Proserpinam] dicit significare fecunditatem seminum: quae cum defuisset quodam tempore, eademque sterilitate terra moereret, exortam esse opinionem, quod filiam Cereris, id est ipsam fecunditatem, quae proserpendo Proserpina dicta esset, Orcus abstulerat, et apud inferos detinuerat: quae res cum fuisset luctu publico celebrata, quia rursus eadem fecunditas rediit, Proserpina reddita exortam esse laetitiam, et ex hoc solemnia constituta." But see also the same text, col. 213, where St. Augustine at some length discusses Proserpine's other characteristic function as wife of Pluto in the Underworld and hence a symbol of death. A copy of the *De Civitate* (Freiburg, 1494) with commentary by Thomas Waleys and Nicholas Trivet, now in the Notre Dame library, presents alongside the basic text a summary of the Proserpine myth with the note, "ex Ovidio" (Bk. VI, C.XX). If Chaucer knew a similar version of the *De Civitate*, his use of Ovid to "complete" Claudian's unfinished account in the *De Raptu* would be a matter of proof; yet, is this necessary for so well-known an author as Ovid? Chaucer's references to St. Augustine's *De Civitate* are: *LGW*, 1690–91; *Parson's Tale*, 532 and 754: in the last mentioned, Chaucer specifies, "Augustinus, de Civitate, libro nono." The alternate conclusion, if Chaucer did not read the *De Civitate*, is that he cites an important text of the middle ages without having read it himself, or without recalling its specific relevance when he wrote the *Merchant's Tale*.

even before the ceremony, January's property is first signed over to the bride. The marriage feast and the uneventful first night further resemble Claudian's in specific details. Once married, May quickly seeks relief from the old man so unlike herself: just as by cunning Proserpine gains the Upperworld, so by cunning May is prepared to enjoy the love of the youthful Damyan; like Pluto, January is offered as a duped husband.

In the Pear-tree Story, January and May continue to contrast like Life and Death, one helped by Pluto and the other by Proserpine. These deities are now transformed into fairies, in accordance with an understandable tradition which reckons as devils all false gods, whatever the mythology in which they originate. Pluto and Proserpine, who seem to be placed in such a setting as Chaucer earlier conceived Parnassus to be, are the living realization of Jupiter's decree, forecast in Claudian and stated as a fact in Ovid. This, we know, allows Ceres' daughter freedom above the Underworld during the fertile months of the year, but, according to Chaucer, in a kind of paradise. The most significant point in the Pear-tree Story to suggest Claudian as more than a reference for collateral reading is Chaucer's dependence on Pluto and Proserpine as "beneficent" deities to help January and May rather than any of the agents given in the analogues.

Since Pluto and Proserpine immediately suggest *feend*-like agents /60/ —Proserpine is such by association with Pluto—one is left with the impression that January, helped by Pluto, and May, by Proserpine, are intended as characters to exemplify the Merchant's text in his special prologue:[14]

> I have a wyf, the worste that may be;
> *For thogh the feend to hire ycoupled were,*
> *She wolde hym overmacche, I dar wel swere.*

This interpretation would not only prepare the reader to meet the incredible depravity of January's life, but would also contribute to an understanding of the Merchant himself. Chaucer causes the Merchant to represent his absent wife as May's equal in cunning and at the same time, ironically, to objectify his own confession of sensuality, to amend for which, we may conjecture, he is making his pilgrimage, only "monthes two" after his marriage.

---

[14] G. G. Sedgewick, "The Structure of the *Merchant's Tale*," *University of Toronto Quarterly*, XVII (1947–48), 340, noted generally that this tale "cannot be properly read apart from" its special prologue. The evidence of this article would support his statement.

Paul A. Olson

Chaucer's Merchant and January's "Hevene in Erthe Heere"[*]

The Merchant in the *Canterbury Tales* tells the tale of a husband whose misfortunes bear an obvious relation to his own marital pain. He has this advantage over his character: that he is perfectly clear-eyed about the miseries of his marriage. One cannot say so much for January. Though the knowledge that one is not "in the perpetual possession of self-deception" may form small consolation if one is a husband in the Merchant's situation, it does seem to dull his affliction somewhat to imagine a character who endures his own extremities but endures with the torpor and innocence of the ass. He would have one believe that he is, unlike January, a man who learns from experience. Thus, January's inner blindness would appear to mirror both the narrator's own past condition and his present contempt for it. However, though the Merchant is clearly conscious of his tale's relevance to the blindness of marital concupiscence, he reveals that some of January's torpor is also his in that he is innocent of its further relevance to his personal position as merchant.

One theme which finds consistent iterative expression throughout the *Canterbury Tales* is the theme of the evil of avarice. Among the harshest words of Dame Prudence is a warning against covetousness as the root of evil (VII, 1836–42; VII, /204/ 1550–1646).[1] Chaucer's good Parson comes down heavy on the same sin (X, 738 ff.). What is expressed in a hortatory fashion in the prose treatises is dramatized with force in the tales: the Summoner's friar goes wrong through the love of money as does the Friar's summoner; the worlds of the Reeve and the Shipman are driven foolish by it; the Canon's Yeoman has his autobiographical tale of what the alche-

---

[*] Reprinted from the *Journal of English Literary History*, XXVIII (September, 1961), 203–214, by permission of the author and The Johns Hopkins Press. ©1961 by The Johns Hopkins Press.
[1] *The Poetical Works of Chaucer*, ed. F. N. Robinson (Cambridge, 1933). All quotations and citations from this edition.

mist's love of gold can do to one, and the Pardoner's revellers are killed by the *radix malorum*, at the foot of the tree whose root is gold. However, the *Merchant's Tale*, told by the representative of the class commonly and possibly justly regarded as most guilty of the vice, says nothing directly concerning the subject. Chaucer, it is true, glances at the Merchant's usury and cleverness in business in the *General Prologue*, but he appears to allow his character, when he speaks in his own voice, to avoid all mention of his business or its motives. This failure to touch the question is the more strange in view of January's being an old man and a Lombard. Old men were characteristically afflicted with the vice of avarice as were supposedly also those Lombards known to most fourteenth century Englishmen. However, the failure to open up the subject is not a lapse if one considers the character who is speaking, and it becomes a positive success if one considers how he speaks. The poet's merchant is a secretive businessman, prudent lest he reveal too much of himself. He could hardly speak of his own business and its vices in the brazen fashion of the Pardoner or the Canon's Yeoman. Even when he tells what he knows about marriage, he only does so by referring to another man's experience. However, that other man of whom he speaks becomes the mirror not only of what his marriage has been but of what he has been and of what his values have been. January's love of May reflects, in heightened colors, the face of his own commercial love of the world's goods.

The shift from the love of a woman to the love of possessions required no very great leap of imagination in medieval times, since, to the medieval mind, the acquisitive vices were essentially matters of love: "Avarice ... is a likerousnesse in herte to have erthely thynges," the Parson asserts (X, 740). Medieval thinkers knew that the desire to possess a woman and the desire to possess any other purely physical object proceeded from the /205/ same root.[2] Thus, by a quite natural transition, January's love of May can become a speculum in which the implications of all possessive desire may be seen. Amid the humid preparations for January's marriage, one point emerges with clarity; January does not love May as a person but as a thing. Her characterization is so flat as hardly to make her a person at all, and there is little evidence that January ever sees her as more than a convenient possession, as even so much as a flat character. As the story

---

[2] The words "libido," "amor," and "concupiscentia" are commonly used in definitions of avarice; cf. "amor habendi," *Aeneid*, VIII, 327, cited by Gerson, *Opera Omnia* (Basil, 1728), I, 338; Arator, *PL*, LXVIII, 131; John Bromyard, *Summa Praedicantium* (Venice, 1586), I, 79ᵛ. For examples of *libido* and *concupiscentia*, cf. Richard Fitzralph, "De Pauperie Salvatoris," in Wyclif's *De Dominio Divino*, ed. Reginald Poole (London, 1890), II, XXV; St. Jerome, *PL*, XXII, 418; called "nutrix luxuriae," Ambrose, *PL*, XIV, 732. The whole fifth book of the *Confessio Amantis* interprets avarice in terms of the metaphor of sexual love. The word "cupiditas" can, of course, mean both avarice and lust in general.

develops, she is surrounded, by an extended submerged comparison, with all the romantic associations of a piece of property. At the outset, the Merchant, in his ironic paraphrasis of January's view of marriage, calls a wife the "fruyt" of a man's treasure (IV, 1270), a permanent gift of God which will outlast the gifts of Fortune and outstay one's desire that she remain (IV, 1311 ff.), a guarantee against adversity, and the "kepere of . . . housbondrye" (IV, 1338, 1380).[3] The speech makes a woman as useful as an insurance policy. Then for January, a woman is as attractive as a delicate calf; she is the "tendre veel" (IV, 1420) which can be bought young for an old man's palate. His woman he purchases after he has examined her and other like fillies in the "commune market-place" of his mind (IV, 1580 ff.), and we are led to believe that he paid to obtain her the good price of feoffment with his land and his real estate in town and tower (IV, 1698, 2172). Such allusions hardly bear out January's reminder to May that he chose her "noght for no coveitise, douteless" (IV, 2166). While it is evident that he did not marry her for her money or property (he had no need of these), it is also evident that he married her *as* money and *as* property, as the last luxury of a prosperous lifetime. January's implicit motives become patent when he becomes jealous, for jealousy, like avarice, is /206/ essentially a possessive vice. To the medieval mind, the husband who locks up his wife is like a miser locking away his treasure; his wife is that treasure, and the gallant who invariably gets at the treasure has something in common with the ordinary thief.[4] The blind and fearful January who clings to his wife with one hand and clutches in

---

[3] I follow Sedgewick in regarding IV, 1267–1392 as the "stream which has been passing through the mind of January"; G. G. Sedgewick, "The Structure of *The Merchant's Tale*," *UTQ*, XVII (1948), 341.

[4] Chaucer's colleague, Gower, is very explicit about this convention: "Bot finali to taken hiede, / Men mai wel make a liklihiede / Betwen him which is averous / Of gold and him that is jelous / Of love, for in on degre / Thei stonde bothe, as semeth me. / That oon wolde have his bagges stille, / And noght departen with his wille, / And dar noght for the thieves slepe, / So fain he wolde his tresor kepe; / That other mai noght wel be glad. / For he is evere more adrad / Of these lovers that gon aboute, /In aunter if thei putte him oute. / So have thei bothe litel joye / As wel of love as of monoie." *Confessio Amantis*, V, 595–610. *The Complete Works of John Gower*, ed. G. C. MacCaulay (Oxford, 1899). The same association, in *La Roman de la Rose*, explains *Amis'* grouping of the sins of *La Jaloux* with the sins of avarice which have beset civilization since the Golden Age. *Le Roman de la Rose*, ed. Ernest Langlois (Paris, 1914–1942), 8355–9664. Jean de Meun's source may have been Alanus who writes concerning the avaricious man: "Sic casus varios terroris somnia monstrant. / Uxoris fraudes, furisque sophismata, terror / Nuntiat. . . ." Alanus de Insulis, "De Planctu Naturae," *PL*, CCX, 446. The convention is evident in the Provencal *Roman de Flamenca*; cf. Paul A. Olson, "*Le Roman de Flamenca*: History and Literary Convention," *SP*, LV (1958), 11, 16–17. It would appear to inform a number of the fabliaux where the jealous husband is also an avaricious member of the bourgeois classes: "Miles Gloriosus," *La "Comedie" Latine en France au*

the other the key to the garden where he can lock her up is certainly more than the Merchant's victim; he is also *moral image* of that prudent and secretive magnate.

January loves May not only as a treasure but as a paradise, and he loves her best in the self-made garden paradise which somehow magnifies her beauty. Any culture's paradise is the visible embodiment of its system of values: its conception of what constitutes man's *summum bonum*. The first thing January announces when he speaks in the tale, is that marriage is so comfortable that it is a *paradise in this world* (IV, 1264–65). The Merchant's paraphrasis of January's views again reminds us that a woman is, indeed, an Eden (IV, 1332). When January chooses a woman, he chooses her as a *heaven*, as a *summum bonum* which carries with it certain other values and liabilities: /207/

> Yet is ther so parfit felicitee
> And so greet ese and lust in mariage,
> That evere I am agast now in myn age
> That I shal lede now so myrie a lyf,
> So delicat, withouten wo and stryf,
> That I shal have *my hevene in erthe heere.* (Italics mine)
> For sith that verray hevene is bought so deere
> With tribulacion and greet penaunce,
> How sholde I thanne, that lyve in swich pleasaunce
> As alle wedded men doon with hire wyvys,
> Come to the blisse ther Crist eterne on lyve ys?
> $\qquad$ (IV, 1641–52)

Knowing what the heavenly paradise costs and what the earthly, January chooses the easier bargain. When aphrodisiacs and hard work do not give him all he hoped to find in this purchased Eden, he builds an external paradise to complement the subjective paradise he found in May, a paradise where complete ownership is possible:

> He made a gardyn, walled al with stoon;
> So fair a gardyn woot I nowher noon . . . .
> In somer seson, thider wolde he go,
> And May his wyf, and no wight but they two;

XII Siecle, ed. Gustav Cohen (Paris, 1931), I, 195 ff.; "De la Borgoise d'Orliens," "De la Dame qui fist batre son mari," "Des Braies au Cordelier," "Aloul," *Recueil Général et Complet des Fabliaux des XIII et XIV Siècles,* ed. M. A. Montaiglon and Gaston Raynaud (Paris, 1872–1890), I, 116 ff.; IV, 133 ff.; III, 275 ff.; I, 255 ff. The convention also informs a number of Renaissance characters who are both avaricious and jealous: Spenser's Malbecco, Shakespeare's Iago, Jonson's Corvino, Security, Fitzdottrell, etc.

>   And thynges whiche that were nat doon abedde,
>   He in the gardyn parfourned hem and spedde.
>   (IV, 2029, 2052)

This garden makes a comfortable world. There all summer things con-
spire to give the feeling that the place is beyond morality: a world perpetually green, perpetually temperate, and perpetually prurient, built in
mimicry and scorn of the "verray Paradise" of *Genesis* with its arbors and
flowing waters. If the first Eden was the Paradise of divine love, this is the
paradise of earthly lust. To get full use of his purchase, January erects a
locus consistent with her kind of value, and, not inappropriately, he lo-
cates at its center a phallic tree of life: the pear tree.[5] /208/ Whether January's garden be considered literally, as a sexual Eden, or figuratively, as
the Eden of the economic man, the Priapean pear tree which crowns it is a
fit summit for a world whose perfections appear as perfections only because they satisfy the desire for acquisition and comfort. Such a pear-tree
Paradise forms an appropriate setting for the consummation of the "temporal marriage" which exists between January and May even as the analogous Garden in one of Chaucer's sources, Deschamps' *Miroir de Mariage*,
with its Fountain of Compunction in the Valley of Humility, its rose of
martyrdom and lily of chastity, is proper to the quiet splendor of "spiritual" marriage.[6] January's phallic garden gives tangible form to the commercial ideal of a "hevene in erthe heere"; Chaucer understood both the
ideal and its splendors.

January's love of May is like the love of possession; it is the love of
possession not as one among many goods but as the highest good. Once
we see the love relationship as bearing this figurative extension, the meaning of the tale's action with respect to its narrator becomes fairly evident.
Wherever May is involved, prosperity is also involved at a secondary level.
January's naive Jovinian arguments in favor of marriage as the font of
happiness constitute ironic arguments in favor of wealth as the spring of

---

[5] *Pirum* is a phallic pun in the "Lydia" (*La "Comedie" Latine*, I, 245) as is "poire"
in Thibaut's *Li Romanz de la Poire* [ed. Friedrich Stehlich (Halle, 1881), pp. 45–47].
An illumination in the ms. of Thibaut's romance shows the pear tree with Cupid sitting
in it, supervising the strategems of a pair of young lovers (Bibl. Nat. Fr. 2186, fol. 15).
The pear's association with the male genitalia and with amorous affairs in general is
based on the double meaning which both "pirum" and "poire" bear; both mean pear
and rod. This double meaning explains the irony of May's line, "so soore longeth me /
To eten of the smale peres grene (IV, 2332–33)." At one level, May is flattering January
with the happy suggestion that she is pregnant; at another, she is suggesting exactly
where her hunger for Damyan is directed; cf. Milton Miller, "The Heir in the *Merchant's Tale*," *PQ*, XXIX (1950), 437–40.

[6] "Le Miroir de Mariage," *Oeuvres Complètes de Eustache Deschamps*, ed. Gaston
Raynaud (Paris, 1894), ll. 6119, 7202–7215.

happiness (IV, 1252–1468) ; the debates concerning whether and how January should undertake marriage also dispute what constitutes man's ultimate good: temporal comfort or spiritual beatitude (IV, 1479–1576, 1617–1690). The marriage binds January to the former good as a reality, and the rest of the story is an experiment in living with this good. That January's end is figuratively connected with the ideal which he has pursued was first noticed by Lydgate who advised his readers to take the tale seriously: "Remembre wele on olde January / Which maister Chaunceres / ful seriously descryvethe, / . . . and how Justyne did vary, / Fro placebo, but yet the olde man wyvethe; / Thus sone he wexeth blynde & than onthryvethe / Fro worldly joye for he sued bad doctryne . . ."[7] Lydgate saw that the story is about /209/ the pursuit of worldly joy, the search for a heaven on earth; he also saw that the first part of the story concerns itself with January's achieving of worldly joy, the last with his losing of it; the two together constitute a typically Boethian action.

In Chaucer's translation of Boethius' *Consolation of Philosophy*, Fortune is the metaphor for temporal goods; her turning represents their necessary variance between seasons of prosperity and seasons of adversity.[8] Reason, whose hope transcends the variabilia of the seen world and seeks the eternal, regards Fortune's frown as cause neither for despair nor for escape. Rather it sees temporal adversity as an aspect of a Providence which, in taking away the ephemera, purifies the good and punishes the wicked, reminding the latter of the insufficiency and impermanency of their goals. By trusting in the eternal, the reasonable man places himself beyond susceptibility to injury from Fortune and her changes. The fool of Fortune is not so protected. Having placed his reliance on the permanence of his temporal prosperity, he is likely to see the loss of that prosperity as the loss of the ultimately valuable. His loss is not the result of destiny or chance. He, of free choice, made himself a candidate for deception by regarding as permanent what must by its nature change. Having chosen to satisfy himself in the transient, material world, his happiness then becomes dependent on the necessity which moves through

---

[7] *Lydgate's Minor Poems*, ed. J. O. Halliwell (London, 1840), p. 28. The poem has sometimes been assigned to Hoccleve.

[8] The tale's conception of prosperity, adversity, and Fortune (IV, 2057), as well as Justinus' conception of the providential implications of suffering (IV, 1655 ff.) are Boethian. Robinson points other Boethian parallels (IV, 1582, IV, 1783 ff.) The tale's indebtedness to the *Consolation of Philosophy* is more a matter of the pattern of its action than of strict verbal echoes, however. Critics recently have questioned the extent to which Chaucer acceded to Boethian conceptions of the freedom of the will; there can be little doubt as to how the *Merchant's Tale* answers this question. Chaucer dramatizes January's choosing between alternatives presented to him by his own speculation and by Placebo and Justinus about as clearly as such choice can be dramatized in a work of art.

transient things. His fall may come with a comic or tragic inevitability, but inevitable it is. Chaucer's *Merchant's Tale* sees the quest for an earthly paradise through the eyes of such Boethian philosophy. In selecting May as his earthly good, January fixes himself to Fortune's wheel by convincing himself of the "permanency" of a delicacy which we know from the beginning must by her nature change. In the garden, he rises to a heaven of wet prosperity; blinded, he begins his fall, and, cuckolded, he ignores the spiritual meaning of an adversity which is no less real for /210/ being comic. Each of these stages in the wheel's turn needs to be analyzed separately.

Adam, according to the Monk, was the first of the human heroes to trust to Fortune and discover his Paradise lost.[9] Deschamps makes Adam a type of the reason, and Eve, a type of the temporal appetites (*M. de M.*, 6991–7039). The *Merchant's Tale* places another of Fortune's heroes in a Paradise with an Eve-like May to govern him through his lower appetites. In the first part of the tale, January considers the arguments of "Raphael" and the "serpent": Justinus and Placebo; St. Jerome and Jovinianus. He is free to choose either. Given the alternatives of Fortune's temporal or Christ's eternal Paradise, he decides for the former. Having made "holynesse" a front for "dotage," he then lets his lower appetites decide for him in the lovely bedroom farce where May is "apoynted" at the direction of an autoerotic dream after her lover has engaged in some curious "bisynesse":

> And whan that he on hire was condescended,
> Hym thoughte his choys myghte nat ben amended.
>
> (IV, 1605–06)

At the beginning, May is a picture in the mind. When January goes blind, she becomes again only a picture to his inner sight, but seen from beneath the pear tree she is, in a confused way, both picture and reality though the desirable imagination ultimately conquers the rather unsatisfactory real thing in January's mind. May's glamor is located primarily in January's fancy; she is most comforting, most paradisal, when she is an illusion. The fact that she is mainly illusion for January both places her firmly among the gifts of Fortune and points up the irony of the Merchant's assertion:

> Alle othere manere yiftes hardily,
> As londes, rentes, pasture, or commune,
> Or moebles, alle been yiftes of Fortune,

---

[9] D. W. Robertson, "Chaucerian Tragedy," *ELH*, XIX (1952), 9–11; my general indebtedness to Professor Robertson is, I hope, apparent.

> That passen as a shadwe upon a wal.
> But drede nat, if pleynly speke I shal,
> A wyf wol laste, and in thyn hous endure,
> Wel lenger than thee list, paraventure.
>
> (IV, 1312–1318)

Whatever other wives may be, January's May is a shadow. /211/

In the garden, January rises up to a heaven of prosperity. At the marriage, he had become the subject of Fortune as well as of Venus; he knows the satisfaction of sexual prosperity, clumsily in the bedroom and then more professionally in the garden: "Ther nys no werkman, whatsoever he be, / That may bothe werke wel and hastily (IV, 1832–1833)." At the same time as he fixes up the enclosed paradise which will insure his felicity, he also manifests his wealth in the luxury of his menage (IV, 2021–2041). The blindness brings to him the first sign that his stock is unsteady (IV, 2057–2068), but, instead of reading the omen and turning, he intensifies his efforts to protect himself from the "poverty" which it forebodes by locking his hand to his wife, and, though blindness temporarily qualifies his sense of security, he is still able to worship in Fortune's paradise with the lush ceremony of genuine religion:

> "Rys up, my wyf, my love, my lady free!
> The turtles voys is herd, my dowve sweete;
> The wynter is goon with alle his reynes weete.
> Com forth now, with thyne eyen columbyn!
> How fairer been thy brestes than is wyn!
> The gardyn is enclosed al aboute;
> Com forth, my white spouse! out of doute
> Thou hast me wounded in myn herte, O wyf!
> No spot of thee ne knew I al my lyf.
> Com forth, and lat us taken oure disport;
> I chees thee for my wyf and my confort."
>
> (IV, 2138–2148)

Fortune's phallic Eden becomes the old man's church, May his Blessed Virgin, and, with a brilliant poetic stroke, the *Sponsus* of Solomon's garden is replaced by deities more conformable to the commercial ideal:[10]

---

[10] The specific interpretation of the *Canticum* which January is inverting is that of St. Jerome, "Adversus Jovinianum" *PL*, XXIII, 263–265. The *Sponsus* is there interpreted as Christ, the *Sponsa* as the Church. The coming of Spring is interpreted as connoting the passage of the old law and the coming of the new, and the other images of the passage are related to various forms of chaste love and love for God. In announcing the coming of "Spring," January is perhaps figuratively announcing the appearance of a new religious dispensation, the commercial dispensation.

Pluto, the god of avarice,[11] and Proserpina, /212/ the goddess of wealth.[12]

January, when cuckolded, ignores the providential meaning of temporal adversity. The same marriage ceremony which gives January his wealth also gives him his poverty; the Venus of earthly love who burns him also burns Damyan,[13] and the mechanical laws which produce the miser create the thief. Damyan's sickness, May's frustration and her pity of Damyan, January's blindness, the whole march of absurd adversity follow mechanically.

The culminating scene is, of course, the great pear-tree scene which, by any standards, must be one of the great comic scenes of literature. While Pluto, as god of avarice and January's sponsor, and Proserpina, as Pluto's possession and May's sponsor, argue with ample Biblical authority concerning the pains of marriage and "ownership," Damyan climbs the

---

[11] Chaucer would have known this convention from Dante (*Inferno*, VII, 1 ff.). Claudius also associates Pluto with riches: Claudius Claudianus, *The Rape of Proserpina*, ed. with translation R. M. Pope (London, 1934), p. 6 (I, 20 ff.), p. 52 (II, 285 ff.). Cf. *Commento di Francesco da Buti sopra La Divina Comedia*, ed. Crescentino Giannini (Pisa, 1858), I, 201; Benvenuto da Imola, *Comentum Super Dantis Aldigherij Comoediam*, ed. W. W. Vernon and J. P. Lacaita (Florence, 1887), I, 243–244; *L'Ottimo Commento della Divina Commedia* (Pisa, 1827), I, 107–108; *Commento alla Divina Commedia d'Anonimo Fiorentino del Secolo XIV*, ed. Pietro Fanfani (Bologna, 1866), I, 179; Pietro Alighieri, *Super Dantis Comoediam Commentarium*, ed. V. Nannucci (Florence, 1845), pp. 96–97; Giovanni Boccaccio, *Il Comento alla Divina Commedia*, ed. Domenico Guerri (Bari, 1918), II, 229–31. From the allegorical tradition which identified Pluto as the god of riches evolved the conception of Pluto as also the god of the avaricious: cf. Fulgentius, *Opera*, ed. R. Helm (Leipzig, 1898), p. 20; *Les Oeuvres Poétiques de Baudri de Bourgueil*, ed. Phyllis Abrahams (Paris, 1926), p. 275; "Mythographus Tertius," *Scriptores rerum mythicarum . . .* , ed. G. H. Bode (Cellis, 1834), p. 174; Giovanni Boccaccio, *Geneologie Deorum Gentilium*, I, 401; Coluccio Salutati, *De Laboribus Herculis*, ed. B. L. Ullman (Zurich, 1951), II, 604.

[12] "Proserpina significat pecuniam," *Two Medieval Satires on the University of Paris*, ed. Louis Paetow (Berkeley, 1927), p. 250. "A serpendo dicta est Proserpina quia fruges per terram serpunt, et quia quecumque inter divitias reputamus in terra latent, ut aurum, gemme, et cetera huiusmodi, bene sub Proserpine nomine possunt intelligi . . ." Salutati, *De Laboribus Herculis*, II, 604. Boccaccio speaks of "Proserpina, la quale alcuna volta significa 'abbondanza.' " Giovanni Boccaccio, *Il Commento alla Divina Commedia*, II, 231; cf. Boccaccio, *Geneologie Deorum Gentilium*, I, 402. The handling of the figures of Pluto and Proserpina may be further clarified when the glosses on Claudian are published. For an illuminating discussion of Chaucer's debt to Claudian, see Mortimer J. Donovan, "The Image of Pluto and Proserpine in the *Merchant's Tale*," *PQ*, XXXVI (1957), 49–60.

[13] The Venus of IV, 1723 and IV, 1777 is one of the clearest cases in Chaucer of the use of a classical god allegorically. The mundane Venus is interpreted conventionally as a symbol of the stimulus of carnal concupiscence and its after effects, and this is precisely the role which Venus plays in this tale. Cf. Fulgentius. *Opera*, p. 39; Bernard Sylvestris, *Commentum Super Sex Libros Eneidos Virgilii*, ed. G. Reidel (Gryphiswaldae, 1924), p. 9; "Mythographus Tertius," p. 228 ff.; Pietro Alighieri, *Super Dantis Comoediam Commentarium*, pp. 604–605; Giovanni Boccaccio, *Teseida delle Nozze d'Emilia*, ed. Aurelio Roncaglia (Bari, 1941), p. 417.

pear tree. May, like /213/ Eve, takes the small green pears from the serpent (IV, 1786) while January hugs the tree to forestall his thievery.
Again the man is deceived by the woman in the garden, and again his
eyes are opened:

> "Out! help! allas! harrow!" he gan to crye,
> "O stronge lady stoore, what dostow?"
> And she answerde, "Sire, what eyleth yow?"
>   (IV, 2366–2368)

January's eyes are opened, but not to his or to May's guilt or to the
absurdity of his situation, for this is only a mimic fall in a mimic bourgeois paradise where failure threatens more than evil because success and
prosperity are everything. Having believed in May as a sound bet in the
way of prosperity, January cannot really believe that he has lost her even
with the evidence at hand. His final absurdity is not that he is cuckolded
but that he does not learn anything in the process, not even anything
about May:

> He kisseth hire, and clippeth hire ful ofte,
> And on hire wombe he stroketh hire ful softe,
> And to his palays hoom he hath hire lad.
>   (IV, 2413–2415)

He imagines a prosperity where none is in order to keep secure an Eden
which never really existed. Thus, as acquisitive man, January makes himself inaccessible to the providential meaning of adversity—that it may be
" 'Goddes meene and Goddes whippe' (IV, 1671) "—by denying what his
eyes tell him in order to believe his wife, that is, in order to believe what
his appetites wish religiously to believe.

Through the Merchant's metaphors, through his references to Boethius,
the Bible, St. Jerome, and the classics, references which are, incidentally,
dramatically inappropriate to him, Chaucer is able to illuminate the
inner fragility of his character's bourgeois world of banking, usury, and
commerce in wools. The Merchant has a wife who like May has deceived
him, a wife who is a figure for the wealth which has seduced him into
usury, avarice, and sophistry (I, 270–284) and yet left him a debtor (I,
280).[14] The Merchant has some advantage over January: the advantage
that he is partly aware that he has been deceived. The knowledge has
/214/ left him cynical and capable only of imagining an experience more
empty than his own and of valuing that experience at the market place

---

[14] I accept the traditional reading of this line; that is, that it implies that the
Merchant is in debt.

rate. The whole section dealing with the Merchant turns on a series of parallelisms: the Merchant and his money; the Merchant and his wife; January and May; Pluto and Proserpina. Each pair is emblematic of unreasonable possessor and unreasonably possessed. In each case, possessor is opposed to possessed as death to life. Altogether the pairs extend Chaucer's satire from the particulars of his own time to classical and universal archetypes which are broader than their particular manifestations in any one historical period.

The *Merchant's Tale* follows directly on the Clerk's. While the *Clerk's Tale* is set in an agrarian, feudal and ultimately religious Italy, the *Merchant's Tale* is set in a prosperous, mercantile, half pagan, and secular Italy. The *Clerk's Tale* is an allegory of spiritual marriage (IV, 1142–1162) ; its purpose is to dramatize that, given certain conditions, suffering and adversity can be meaningful. The *Merchant's Tale* is a tale of a temporal marriage; its action evidences that there is a world in which even prosperity is meaningless: the world beyond the morality of the economic man. The two worlds, the world of Griselda and the world of January, lie side by side in the *Canterbury Tales* as they lay side by side in fourteenth-century England and fourteenth-century Italy and as they were to lie for the next four centuries. Chaucer's comment on one of those worlds is not less clear eyed and impersonal and perfect than Jonson's or Swift's or Blake's. The *Merchant's Tale* bears implications which reach in many directions; one of those directions is the vision of good which compels the acquisitive society.

Gertrude M. White

"Hoolynesse or Dotage": The Merchant's January*

Until a few years ago, "The Merchant's Tale" was traditionally viewed in the dramatic context of the Marriage Group, as an extreme statement of the "wo that is in mariage,"[1] and one end of a spectrum of attitudes toward matrimony, the other of which is furnished by "The Franklin's Tale." Apart from this, critical comment centered, with some distaste, on the gross bawdiness of the narrative and the cold savagery of the narrator. Recent scholarship has begun to see the tale from a different angle, to emphasize depths and dimensions only hinted at by earlier scholars, and to explore in some detail allegorical and symbolical elements.[2] It is my intention in this paper to consider the exact nature of the wider, more meaningful and serious frame of reference in the Tale, particularly as it is embodied in the character of January and in the Merchant's attitude toward him.

It has been a truism of criticism that the Merchant's savagery is directed not merely at January but at himself. "It is a case of seeing a blinded

* Reprinted from *Philological Quarterly*, XLIV (July, 1965), 397–404, by permission of the author and The University of Iowa.

1 "The Wife of Bath's Tale," *The Works of Geoffrey Chaucer*, ed. F. N. Robinson (Cambridge, 1957), p. 76, line 3. All citations from Chaucer in my text are from this edition.

2 See especially the following articles: Bertrand H. Bronson, "Afterthoughts on 'The Merchant's Tale,'" *Studies in Philology*, LVIII (1961), 596; J. A. Burrow, "Irony in 'The Merchant's Tale,'" *Anglia*, LXXV (1957), 199–208; Mortimer J. Donovan, "The Image of Pluto and Proserpine in 'The Merchant's Tale,'" *Philological Quarterly*, XXXVI (1957), 49–60; Philip Griffith, "Chaucer's 'Merchant's Tale,'" *Explicator*, XVI (1957), No. 13; Alfred L. Kellogg, "Susannah and 'The Merchant's Tale,'" *Speculum*, XXXV (1960), 275–79; William W. Main, "Chaucer's 'Merchant's Tale,'" *Explicator*, XIV (1955), No. 13; Paul A. Olson, "Chaucer's Merchant and January's 'Hevene in Erthe Heere,'" *English Literary History*, XXVIII (1961), 203–14; D. W. Robertson, "The Doctrine of Charity in Medieval Literary Gardens," *Speculum*, XXVI (1951), 24–49; G. G. Sedgewick, "The Structure of 'The Merchant's Tale,'" *University of Toronto Quarterly*, XVII (1948), 337–45.

sensualist through the eyes of a sensualist who is awakened and embittered."[3] Himself disillusioned by personal experience, the Merchant
tells the story of a ridiculous and repulsive dotard foolish enough to
believe that wives are true and wedlock a paradise. /398/

This is true so far as it goes. But it does not sufficiently account for the
ironic power and moral weight of the Tale. "The Pardoner's Tale," alone
among the Tales of Canterbury, approaches it in these respects. And recent critical studies, perceiving the essential seriousness of "The Merchant's Tale," have emphasized its "drift toward allegory,"[4] its "mimic
fall in a mimic bourgeois paradise,"[5] and declared that its aim, like that
of so much medieval literature, is to "promote Charity and to condemn
Cupidity,"[6] to show the vanity of seeking a heaven upon earth.

In this view of the Tale, January is the type of the blind materialist,
and his garden, the scene of his own lust and that of May and Damyan, is
seen to be linked with other gardens and filled with echoes of other loves,
holy and unholy. It is Susannah's garden, the scene of the Elders' lust;[7]
Parnassus, the pagan terrestrial paradise, traditional home of the gods;[8]
the garden of the *Roman de la Rose*, with its ideal of courtly love;[9] the
garden of Deschamps' *Miroir de Mariage*, a spiritual paradise;[10] the garden of the "Song of Songs," representing the holy love between Christ
and His Church.[11] The allegorical implications are strengthened by the
names of the characters, by January's blindness, and by such obvious
correspondences as exist between Pluto and January, May and Proserpine, each pair "emblematic of the unreasonable possessor and the unreasonably possessed."[12]

If one looks at the Tale from this viewpoint, it will be seen that the
Merchant, however clear-eyed about marriage, is as blind as old January
to the fundamental illusion involved and to the relevance of the tale to
his own personal position. The two men have something in common besides "wo in mariage." Both are wholly committed to the world and the
flesh. But Chaucer, we know, was not. "Repeyreth hom fro worldly
vanyte," he had advised "yonge, fresshe folkes" at the end of the "Troilus"
(lines 1835–37). Shot through as it is with the teller's bitter contempt

---

[3] Sedgewick, p. 343.
[4] Burrow, p. 203.
[5] Olson, p. 213.
[6] Robertson, p. 24.
[7] Kellogg, p. 9.
[8] Donovan, p. 13.
[9] Compare Burrow and Robertson, above.
[10] John C. McGalliard, "Chaucer's 'Merchant's Tale,' and Deschamps' Miroir de Mariage,'" *Philological Quarterly*, XXV (1946), 193–220.
[11] Kellogg, p. 10.
[12] Olson, p. 214.

for an old dupe, the tale, according to this interpretation, is given its ultimate meaning by a philosophy wholly alien both to January and to the /399/ Merchant. If the key to January's character, as has been claimed,[13] is "fantasye" or illusion, the illusion embraces more than the nature of marriage: it includes the whole of life.

We are thus invited, in effect, to consider "The Merchant's Tale" from two different angles. They are not, to be sure, mutually exclusive, but differ in emphasis; in their conception of where the Tale's center of gravity is to be found. The traditional view is that a disgruntled victim is indulging in a bitterly brilliant exposé of women and marriage, and holding up to invincible ridicule an old dupe who is taken in by both. The other, more recent view, is that the true meaning of the tale lies deeper; that it is a somewhat different kind of exemplum which, under the guise of realistic fabliau, is actually a sermon on the blindness and error of materialism. But there is a third possible angle from which the Tale may be viewed, and one which more fully accounts for two things which seem to me to demand further consideration: the element of pathos which emerges ever and again in the presentation of January, and which is as real though not as obvious as his repulsiveness; and the chilling savagery of the Merchant's attitude toward him, which the self-identification, self-confession motif does not seem to me adequate to explain.

The key to January's character is "fantasye" indeed. It is the exact nature of his fantasy which needs to be further explored. Now, the very first thing we learn about January, that from which all his future troubles are to flow, is that he has experienced a complete reversal of his hitherto lifelong behavior and attitude. The first few lines of the tale put us in possession of the situation with swiftness and economy. January is a "worthy knyght" (1246) who has lived wifeless for sixty years "in greet prosperitee; ... And folwed ay his bodily delyt/On wommen ther as was his appetyte." (1247–50). Nothing could more clearly portray an elderly sensualist accustomed to a self-indulgent and conscienceless pursuit of the things of this world. But when he has passed his sixtieth year, with a suddenness and completeness that resemble a religious conversion, he reverses his position and embraces the thought of wedlock with fanatic fervor. The Merchant drily offers a choice of reasons: "Were it for hoolynesse or for dotage/I kan nat seye" (1253–54). It is perfectly obvious, of course, what his choice is, and in all the details of the story he does say. In his eyes, January is a silly old fool. But in what, exactly, does his /400/ silliness consist? Not in the sensuality and materialism characteristic of him earlier. No; precisely in the other term which the Mer-

---

13 Burrow, p. 203.

chant offers: in "hoolynesse." January's self-deception and rationalization
are exhibited in his blindness to holiness, as well as to women and
marriage. It is not simply that he is a materialist who substitutes the
love of earthly things for that of heavenly things, but that he deceives
himself into mistaking the one for the other. He remains a sensualist and
a materialist, as he has always been, but he convinces himself that he is
now seeking the spiritual life. The Merchant sees him, and makes us see
him, as a disgusting and hypocritical old lecher; and so he is; but he is
not a clear-eyed, consistent, and conscious lecher, as he was before. He
has a foot in both worlds. Or rather—hence, perhaps, his name—he is
facing two different ways at the same time. His folly consists as much in
deceiving himself about his real motives and real feelings as in being
deceived by May and Damyan.

At first, January's ambivalence is both amusing and repulsive. He
mixes his modes, as it were, with complete unconsciousness of inconsistency. In his first speech to his friends, announcing his intention of marriage, he glides from spiritual to sensual to practical considerations without changing gears. Opening with the pathetic:

> . . . Freendes, I am hoor and oold,
> And almoost, God woot, on my pittes brynke;
> Upon my soule somwhat moste I thynke,

he continues by stipulating for "som mayde fair and tendre of age," for,
in a very revealing figure, "bet than old boef is the tendre veel" (1420).
Besides, a young wife is more easily controlled than a "womman thritty
yeer of age" (1421) and more apt to bear children. He had rather be
eaten by hounds than have his heritage fall into strange hands—irony
indeed, considering the probable parentage of his "heir"[14]—and procreation besides, he assures his audience, is "to th'onour of God above"
(1449). Then, in a final contradiction of his opening lament:

> For, God be thanked! I dar make avaunt,
> I feele my lymes stark and suffisaunt
> To do al that a man bilongeth to.   (1457–59)

The thing that is most evident about January from the beginning is his
capacity for self-deception. But it is just as obvious that this self-deception takes the specific form of quite unconscious hypocrisy as to his real
feelings and true motives. His materialism and /401/ sensuality are dis-

---

[14] Milton Miller, "The Heir in 'The Merchant's Tale,'" *Philological Quarterly*,
XXIX (1950), 437–40.

guised from his own eyes as "hoolynesse." As the Pardoner said of himself, in another connection: "Thus spitte I out my venym under hewe / Of
hoolynesse, to semen hooly and trewe" (421–22). But unlike the Pardoner, January has not clearly diagnosed his own case. It is this confusion
and ambivalence which account for the extraordinary mixture of the
comic, the repulsive, and the pitiable in his portrait. And as the tale progresses, not only does the mixture become more and more apparent, but
the emphasis shifts. The old fool at whom we have laughed and shuddered
assumes, if only for a fleeting moment or two, the stature of an almost
tragic figure.

At first, ridicule and contempt are dominant. We pass from the rich
comedy of Justinus' ironic reassurances that marriage will not endanger
his eternal salvation by two much earthly bliss, to the blasphemy of "the
hooly sacrement" (1702) invoked on such a union as that of January
and May; his scruples that "thilke nyght offenden hire moste he" (1756)
are coupled with grotesque eagerness for the arrival of the wedding night;
his reassurances that:

> In trewe wedlok coupled be we tweye;
> And blessed be the yok that we been inne,
> For in oure actes we mowe do no synne,   (1836–38)

while ostensibly directed to his wife are necessary for himself; and his
self-satisfaction on the wedding morning is sharply contrasted with the
cruelty of his portrait. As Professor Tatlock says: "That we must needs
despise what should be pitiful fixes the mood."[15] January's garden, pre-
sided over by Priapus, in which ". . . thynges whiche that were nat doon
abedde, / He in the gardyn parfourned hem and spedde" (2051–52),
strengthens repulsion and directs sympathy to May, the object of his
hypocritical and senile lust. And when, stricken by blindness, he reveals
his self-centered and egotistical possessiveness by wishing her perpetual
widowhood after his death, and by literally refusing to let her out of his
grasp, he becomes a wholly contemptible figure.

But selfishness, egotism, and lust are not the whole picture. Now the
emphasis shifts to "hoolynesse" rather than "dotage." Egged on by May,
who has made plans of her own, January invites his wife into the garden
in a lyric passage taken directly from the "Song of Songs." And in the
interpretation of this passage, most commentators on the tale seem to me
to have gone astray.

January's words are not conscious blasphemy. We are, no doubt, /402/
meant to contrast the quality of his love with "the highest love the Middle

---

15 J. S. P. Tatlock, "Chaucer's 'Merchant's Tale,'" *Modern Philology*, XXXIII
(1936), 368.

Ages could conceive."[16] And to the Merchant, that single-minded materialist who can see only the ridiculous and contemptible side of January,
as of women and marriage too, these "words of the Holy Ghost"[17] are
"olde lewed words" (2149). But January is expressing what, in his blind
self-deception, seems to him the truth of his feelings. He is, in fact, echo-
ing the ironic counsel of the Merchant in his mock eulogy of marriage at
the opening of the tale: "Love wel thy wyf, as Crist loved his chirche"
(1384). That his love for May differs from that of Christ for the Church
is easily enough perceived by anyone else; but January, be it remembered, is blind. It is in this very confusion of "dotage" with "hoolynesse"
that his blindness resides. And this is the source of the Merchant's poison-
ous contempt for him.

As the story moves to its ribald dénouement, the element of pathos in
January's plight stands out in bolder relief and lends him a considerable
measure of dignity. His avowal of love—"Levere ich hadde to dyen on a
knyf, / Than thee offende, trewe deere wyf!" (2163)—and plea for her
constancy, even though characteristically he mingles both spiritual and
material inducements—"First, love of Crist, and to yourself honour, /
And al myn heritage, toun and tour" (2171–72)—is set against her
blandly false and blasphemous vow of truth as she signals Damyan to
climb the pear tree. And when she asks January's help in reaching the
pears, he assents in these words: "Certes," quod he, "thereon shal be no
lak, / Mighte I yow helpen with myn herte blood" (2346–47). Only by
deliberately ignoring these plain indications can January be interpreted
as wholly immersed in materialism and sensuality. He is indeed a Janus
figure who faces two different worlds and, being blind, sees neither for
what it is. The cynical Merchant who tells his story lives wholly in the
world of too solid flesh and too frail constancy. And "fresshe" May and
"gentil" Damyan, whom the Merchant regards with such acrid amusement, suffer no pangs of incipient idealism. They know very well who and
what they are, what they want, and how to get it. Damyan's forthright
treatment of the lady in the pear tree furnishes a mordantly comic contrast to January's earlier fears for his bride:

> . . . Allas! O tendre creature,
> Now wolde God ye myghte wel endure
> Al my corage, it is so sharp and keene!
> I am agast ye shul it nat susteene.   (1757–60)/403/

The Merchant's satire is not directed against unblushing and soulless sensuality. Damyan and May are allowed to portray their own degradation

---

16 Kellogg, p. 279.
17 Tatlock, p. 375.

objectively and almost without comment from the narrator. It is January whom the Merchant despises; not because he is a sensualist but because he is a sensualist who has intimations, imperfect as they are, of another world. "Lilies that fester smell far worse than weeds." The lewd comedy of the pear tree seems almost benign beside the "blessed yok" of January's marriage. His belated conversion to holy wedlock, his wedding with its sumptuous splendor, its invocation of all the beauty and dignity of the ancient world, lead only to the grotesque physical ugliness of the wedding morning and to the darker moral ugliness of the unholy garden and his final complete undoing.

Pluto and Proserpine, it has been pointed out, furnish a comic counterpart to January and May both on the narrative and on the allegorical level. They are clearly reminiscent of the Wife of Bath and any one of her five husbands arguing the perennial subject of "The tresons whiche that wommen doon to man," as Pluto puts it (2239), and citing texts and authorities against one another.[18] And certainly Pluto, god of the "dirke regioun / Under the ground," as the Franklin later describes him, possesses his young queen as unreasonably as old January possesses young May.[19] Each desires to help and protect his counterpart. But here, too, the most striking feature of their dialogue is their comic blindness to themselves. Pluto, who passionately identifies with January,[20] sees him only as "this honurable knyght" (2254), this "olde, blynde, worthy knyght" (2259), about to be betrayed by "his owene man" (2256). Proserpine, who is clear-sighted about men—she describes Solomon, to whom her husband has appealed in support of women's "wikkednesse" as "a lecchour and an ydolastre" (2298), terms fully as applicable to January—furnishes the most irresistibly comic note of the whole tale as she continues her indictment of "this Jew, this Salomon" (2277): "So made he eek a temple of false goddis./How myghte he do a thyng that moore forbode is" (2295-96)? The speaker of those lines had, no more than January, the power to see herself as others see her! /404/

It is possible, of course, to overdo symbol, allegory, ambiguity, levels of meaning, and all the sometimes dreary paraphernalia of the modern critical mode. "Chaucer," remarks a contemporary scholar, rather sourly, "was writing a concrete narrative poem, not an allegorical psychomachy."[21] But even a concrete narrative poem, one supposes, is bound to select such characters and events and present them in such a way as to

---

[18] G. L. Kittredge, "Chaucer's Discussion of Marriage," *Modern Philology*, IX (1912), 456.

[19] Olson, p. 214.

[20] Olson suggests that Pluto is, according to Dante, the god of avarice, and thus may be associated with merchants in general and January in particular.

[21] McGalliard, p. 218.

make an implicit comment on the nature of human experience and human life. And so, even apart from more explicit allegory, there remain the great themes of Chaucer's human comedy: the imperfection of human nature, the comic, pathetic, sometimes tragic contrast between the loftiness of human aspirations and the limits of the human condition. And "The Merchant's Tale," with its unforgettable figure of old January, is surely one of his richest and most successful treatments of these themes.

Margaret Schlauch

Chaucer's *Merchant's Tale* and Courtly Love*

The story of January and May, brilliantly and devastatingly told by Chaucer in the *Merchant's Tale*, has recently been the subject of an unusual amount of discussion. As befits a decade inured to the consummate, cynical, and outspoken (if far less kindly) narrative art of Aldous Huxley, contemporary criticism no longer avoids the challenge of this unsparing presentation of human motive. Though some may feel still a profound distaste for the story as such, at least discussion of it is not so commonly avoided now as in an age which demanded reticence and evasion where Chaucer's—and ours—placed no such tabus. The changed temper of our times, and the changed standards concerning appropriate subject matter of literature, no doubt explain some of the increased scholarly interest in this particular tale.

Two articles of major interest have appeared on the subject during the last year. Germaine Dempster has made an exhaustive study of the sources and analogues,[1] which illuminates as never before the course and mutations of this story so eminently unflattering to the human talents for honesty and fidelity. We have long since been aware that the nuclear plot is Oriental in origin; to be reminded of this more circumstantially than ever before is to refresh our understanding of the cultural and historical reasons for its cynicism. No comment is needed at this late date on the prevalently adverse attitude to women in Oriental fiction, and the underlying causes of its condemnatory character. Stories springing from the Orient are apt to retain this attitude even after they have been assimilated

---

* Reprinted from *Journal of English Literary History*, IV (September, 1937), 201–212, by permission of the author and The Johns Hopkins Press. © 1937 by The Johns Hopkins Press.
[1] "On the Source of the Deception Story in the *Merchant's Tale*," Mod. Phil., 34 (1936), 133–54.

in some degree to the different social background and intellectual climate of Europe. Chaucer's *Merchant's Tale* is no exception, even with its setting of late feudalism and courtly love.

There remains the question, however, concerning the appropriateness of using the subject at all. Granted that the plot /202/ was Oriental and therefore prone to mock at woman's constancy, why did Chaucer choose to treat it? Professor Tatlock has posed this question and attempted a reply in the second article to which I refer.[2] In his literary evaluation he emphasizes the savage mood, obscenity, and repellent qualities of the tale, and the presumptive bitterness of the author in composing it. The brilliance and cold intelligence of the narrator's mastery are of course conceded. Chaucer's very savagery in handling the *dramatis personae* is, we are told, an endearing trait: it leaves us in no doubt concerning his attitude to the doting and foolish husband, to sensual May, and spineless Damian. That the threadbare conventions of courtly love served largely for the decking out of that puppet figure, the enamoured squire, is justly recognized and clearly stated. It is with the implications of Professor Tatlock's remarks that I find myself in some disagreement. His statement is trenchant and inclusive:

> But for Damian any interest or sympathy is impossible. He goes through the motions expected in fashionable literature from a youth newly in love; he covets May at once, takes to his bed, writes verses, as to the consumation of his desires merely does as he is bid, and after the exposure leaves the exculpation to May. The timidity and lack of enterprise are here in plenty which seem to have been so attractive to the masterful dame of the later Middle Ages, at least to read about. We infer that he is good-looking and well-bred, but that is all. The male type which Chaucer elaborated with so much sympathy in Troilus, and with tolerant amusement in Aurelius, could not be treated with more negligent indifference than here. His tricks of a dandy and his pleasantness to everyone read like a parody on Chaucer's earlier account of the ennobling effect on Troilus of his happy love . . . If in the *Franklin's Tale* Chaucer had outgrown what is sometimes called the "conventions of courtly love," in the *Merchant's* he arrantly turned against them.

No one will quarrel, I believe, with this characterization of Damian. Isolating the story from the context of Chaucer's other work, we perceive merely a bitter, negative mockery of fashionable convention; relating it to the *Troilus* and *Franklin's Tale* we perceive the measure of Chaucer's change. But I believe that some elucidation is still required on the reasons for that change and, above all, its significance. /203/

---

[2] "Chaucer's *Merchant's Tale*," *Mod. Phil.*, 33 (1936), 367–81.

It is a commonplace to say that the whole fashion of courtly love—as indeed its name indicates—was a prerogative of feudal aristocracy. From the days of the troubadours and the first codification of its rules in the twelfth century, through the age of romances, its exponents made clear repeatedly that the lower orders were disqualified from its practices. This is no matter for surprise, of course. The necessity for the limitation is obvious. If Ydelnesse (to use Chaucer's term) is the guardian of the bright garden of Love whose lord is Mirth, and if Richesse, Largesse, and Fraunchise are among its leading denizens, it is no wonder that entry was limited to a very restricted class. It could not be said of all comers, as of the Dreamer in the *Romance of the Rose*, that the strict portress Ydelnesse (or Leisure, as we should call her)

> dide me so great bountee,
> That she the gate of the gardin
> Undide, and leet me passen in.

When he was translating the *Romance of the Rose*, Chaucer probably accepted this statement without question. But there is evidence that he did not continue to do so throughout his life.

Concerning the exclusiveness of chivalrous love, in fact of all love as we understand it, the first codifier speaks in no uncertain terms. Andreas Capellanus constructs his discussion on the basis of a scheme determined by class distinctions. His *Nobilis* may woo *Nobilior*; even *Plebeius* may approach a *Domina Nobilis* (if he has the income to assure leisure, largesse, mirth, and festivity). Andreas, to be sure, echoes common mediaeval sentiment concerning the true test of nobility: nothing but *probitas et compositio morum*. "Gentilesse" of the heart (to use Chaucer's words) might be regarded as the mark of worth rather than family or aristocratic birth; love may be praised in Biblical language because it raises them that are low and blesses with humility those of high degree; common descent from Adam may lead to the formula *Magis ex moribus quam ex sanguine nobilitas*—yet the fact remains that any *Plebeius* who regarded himself as a candidate for the practice of courtly love would have to possess both the wealth and leisure which its rules require.[3] Shall we say: he might be the son of a wealthy vintner, a wholesale merchant with court connections, like Chaucer's father, but not a petty tradesman, and certainly not an apprentice who lived, slept, and ate in the master's

---

[3] The doctrine of equality among men because of common descent from Adam, and of virtue as a test of the true *gentilesse*, is presented in the famous passage in Chaucer's *WBT*, 1. 1109 ff. Cf. F. N. Robinson's note: "It was a commonplace of Christian literature and in no sense an evidence of radical or advanced opinion on the part of Chaucer." The same is true of Andreas.

work-shop? Even the wealthy *Plebeius,* or member of the third estate, might find his aristocratic mistress, the *Domina Nobilis,* asking him gravely: "What confusion would not your doctrine of the equality of lovers cause in society?" The question appears in the model conversation composed by Andreas under the title *Plebeius Nobili.*

One class was unquestionably excluded from the remotest possibility of participation in the elaborate game of *amour courtois,* namely the peasantry or what may be called in modern language the fourth estate. The words of Andreas on this subject are harshly emphatic. The passage is well known, but its significance for Chaucer's general attitude deserves comment.

> Sed ne id, quod superius de plebeiorum amore tractavimus, ad agricultores crederes esse referendum, de illorum tibi breviter amore subiungimus. Dicimus enim vix contingere posse, quod agricolae in amoris inveniantur curia militare, *sed naturaliter sicut equus* et mulus ad Veneris opera promoventur, quemadmodum impetus eis naturae demonstrat. Sufficit ergo agricultori labor assiduus et vomeris ligonisque continua sine intermissione solatia. Sed, etsi quandoque, licet raro, contingat, *eos ultra sui naturam* amoris aculeo concitari, ipsos tamen in amoris doctrina non expedit erudire, ne, dum actibus sibi *naturaliter* alienis intendunt, humana praedia, illorum solita fructificare labore, cultoris defectu nobis facta infructifera sentiamus.[4]

The contrast is sharp indeed. It is the nature of peasants to love in animal fashion, like a horse; their assiduous and quite uninterrupted labor makes aught else impossible. This labor must be their solace: *solatia* is the very word used for the joys of love in more favored circles. If an *agricultor* should be guilty of the unnatural lapse of loving in the more exalted /205/ sense, it would be most unwise to instruct him in the doctrine of such an emotion, for while he devotes time and attention to the gay science, the economic goods (*humana praedia*) for which we depend on him would not be forthcoming. Andreas could not have made the matter clearer. He concludes with the general counsel that little time should be wasted on the wooing of a peasant girl who has aroused the passing fancy of a man of rank: *si locum inveneris opportunum, non differas assumere, quod petebas et violento potiri amplexu.*

It is true that no student of the institution of chivalry has failed to recognize this fundamental limitation of courtly love, but I do not believe it has been given due importance in tracing Chaucer's changing attitude to the subject. Agnes K. Getty, for instance, has surveyed the course of Chaucer's treatment of the code throughout all of his works, and es-

---

[4] I, ch. 11 (ed. E. Trojel: *Andreae Capellani De Amore Libri tres,* Havniae, 1892, p. 235 f. Italics mine).

tablished a general tendency "to rebel against the conventional concept
of the humble lover"[5]—the type of person who is so mercilessly portrayed
in the Damian of the *Merchant's Tale*. As opposed to the conventional
point of view, she observes in Chaucer an increasing inclination to criti-
cise its artificiality, to satirize it, and to substitute a common sense point
of view. But she does not elucidate the underlying causes of this shift on
Chaucer's part. One of them, I am sure, is his growing awareness of the
limitations of class which Andreas had made baldly clear centuries before.

The *Parliament of Fowles*, as Miss Getty points out, is conspicuous for
its presentation of the non-conforming point of view as well as the traditional one. The "dispute between the water fowl and the other birds is
nothing more or less than an argument for and against the prescribed
conduct of the romantic lover. It is obvious that the dispute is used by
Chaucer as an artistic device to heighten the contrast between the chivalric conception of love and the opposite conception as expressed by the
water fowl. . . ." This opposite conception, undefined except vaguely as a
common sense point of view, is quite clearly affected by the awareness
that love is an aristocratic prerogative. That the groups of birds represent
social classes is generally /206/ admitted. The eagles, who quite clearly
stand for the nobility, insist that the lover to be chosen must be

548   "the worthieste
                        Of knyghthod, . . .
                        Most of estat, of blod the gentilleste";

the water fowl (possibly standing for the rich merchants) say sensibly
and briefly in the person of the goose

566   "I seye I rede him, though he were my brother,
            But she wol love hym, lat hym love another!"

But the treason toward love uttered by the duck evokes a sharp retort
from the aristocratic tercelet, recalling the strictures of Andreas:

596   "Now fly, cherl!" quod the gentil tercelet,
                        "Out of the donghill cam that word ful right!
                        Thou canst nat seen which thyng is wel beset!
                        Thou farst by love as oules don by lyght:
                        The day hem blent, ful wel they se by nyght.
                        Thy kynde is of so low a wrechednesse
                        That what love is, thow canst nat seen ne gesse."

---

[5] "Chaucer's Changing Conceptions of the Humble Lover," *PMLA*, 44 (1929), 202–16.

What is this other than a poetic statement of the principle of Andreas that peasants love *naturaliter sicut equus,* and that a nobler form of the emotion is *ultra sui naturam?* There are other reasons for the humorous and satiric tone of the *PF,* to be sure, but awareness of the limitations of class is surely one of them.

II

In the *Merchant's Tale,* as we have remarked, the satire on the whole system of feudal love is very bitter. It is not only the characters whom Chaucer is willing to condemn as individuals, but in part also their code. The egregiously foolish husband is a knight; the humble lover is a squire presumably training for knighthood. The social *milieu* is precisely that of the conventional romances; the characters are the types omni-present in them.[6] If we give a simplified statement of the situation it might sound like a perfectly serious thirteenth /207/ century French romance: a young squire, serving his feudal lady at table, is suddenly smitten with love for her; he is covered with confusion, develops love-sickness, takes to his bed, and remains ill until he is able to convey his entreaties to her by letter and win a show of kindness from her, despite the vigilance of her guardian (here, her husband). In such a context of conventional narrative the line

Lo, pitee renneth soon in gentil herte!

would not appear disharmonious. If Chaucer gives it an inexpressibly sardonic tone, it is because of his treatment of the entire situation.

The amazing unconventionality of that treatment emerges more clearly than ever before, I believe, if we compare it with one which is externally, at least, quite close in French romance: the account of the enamouring of the hero in *Amadas et Ydoine.* This popular romance, which was certainly well known in England, offers some instructive parallels to the *Merchant's Tale.*[7]

Amadas, like Damian, "carf beforn the knyght ful many a day," for he is the seneschal's son

205	Li senescaus a icel jour
	Sert a la table son seignour . . .
209	Et Amadas devant son pere.

---

[6] Miss Getty says almost nothing about the significance of the *Merchant's Tale* in her study of Chaucer's Humble Lover.

[7] *Amadas et Ydoine,* ed. John R. Reinhard, Paris, 1926. The evidence for its popularity in England is given, p. vi f.

It is while he is in the act of carving for Ydoine that he is so smitten that "almooste he swelte and swowned ther he stood" and was "ny wood" for pain:

279   Pales devint, aval s'acline,
                        Pasmés chiet devant la mescine.

Concerning Damian we are told briefly that "to his bed he wente hym hastily"; Amadas does so not merely once, but on the several occasions when he pleads vainly with Ydoine:

328   Conduit l'en ont a son ostel
                        Et si l'ont coucié en un lit . . .
808   Il a trouvé son lit tout prest;
                        Tous malades couchiés s'i est./208/

The abject behavior of Amadas is exaggerated to a degree which suggests humor even in the French romances. After Ydoine has rejected him for the third time he drags himself across her threshold and, "pour la ramprosne c'a oiee" he swoons once more:

777   Tant est faibles que cuer et cors
                        A la terre est cheiis pasmés;
                        Pales, tains et descoulourés,
                        Tous estendus gist a la tere.

Although Ydoine resists the appeals to "pitee" far longer than the ready and eager May, her capitulation is due to the same motive:

1103   Pitiés et Francise et Paours
                        Forgent mult tost un trencant dart.

Moreover, if May's "excellent franchise" is ironically praised by Chaucer at this point, it is because she too is reluctant to

E 1991   han lat hym sterven in the place
               Wel rather than han graunted hym hire grace;
               And [to] rejoysen in hire crueel pryde,
               And rekke nat to been an homycide.

So with Ydoine. For the same reason she relents (after absurd delays)

1075   Adont primes pités l'em prent;
                        Ne quide avoir confession
                        Ja mais a nul jor ne pardon
                        Dou grant pechié que ele a fait

> *Se ele ensi morir le laist*
> A grant angousse pour s'amour.

The visit of May to Damian's bedside has the same beneficent effect as Ydoine's show of affection to her invalid lover.

E 2009   Up riseth Damyan the nexte morrwe
            Al passed was his sikensse and his sorwe.

and Amadas feels such joy

1304   Que tost revint en sa coulour
           Et cuer et cors li enforcist.
           Tant par amende et embelist,
           Com cil qui a quanque il veut.

There is a further similarity between the situations of Damian and Amadas. In the French romance, the union of the lovers is /209/ long delayed by the presence of Ydoine's husband (imposed upon her against her will in the absence of Amadas). He is presented as a ludicrous person, terrified by a show of witchcraft into complete abstinence from his wife. By this device Ydoine prevents the consummation of the marriage and keeps herself *pucele et pure* for Amadas. The husband's predicament is described with some humor:

2367   Toute voies se va coucier
           La nuit dejouste sa moullier,
           Mais tous est mas et esgarés;
           Mult a corages et pensés:
           Ne set ou le faire ou laissier ...
2378   Faire li veut, mais n'ose pas ...

Comparable to his predicament is that of January, concerning whose lack of potency Chaucer gives such broad and humorous hints. Here again the romance offered a situation which fairly clamored for burlesque.

Other romances, of course, offer a general resemblance to the triangle of January, May, and Damian. *Guy of Warwick* is one of these. It presents a similar exaggeration, to the point of absurdity, of conventional behavior. It may not be that *Amadas et Ydoine* is the specific French courtly romance Chaucer was burlesquing in the *Merchant's Tale*;[8] in fact, no

[8] The names Amadas and Damian are not very close, to be sure; but it is interesting to note that the hero of a romantic Icelandic saga clearly derived from some form of the *Amadas* romance is called Dámusti. (The relation of the *Amadas* and *Dámusta saga* is the subject of a paper read by me before the Scandinavian group of the MLA in December, 1936.)

one model was needed for a plot which makes fun of the most general
tenets of the code of *amour courtois*. But the similarities of detail between *Amadas* and the *Merchant's Tale* are unusually close, and they
sharpen our sense of the effect Chaucer deliberately aimed to produce.

He could not indeed have found a more absurd lover in the whole range
of French romance than Amadas. The mere act of changing a romantic
situation into a *fabliau* implies a critical attitude. The mediaeval *fabliaux*
constitute our antidote for the unsubstantial and sugared fare of the
romances; they present an antithesis of sharp unconscious criticism, and
it is significant that they spring largely from a different class. When the
values /210/ of one type are permitted to intrude in the other, the result
is not only comedy but also social satire, whether deliberate or involuntary. Thus, one of the anonymous humorous tales in Middle High German
tells us of a niggardly bourgeois husband, who was so mean that he locked
up all the food and clothing in his home before he went out each day.
His wife, left alone in the bare rooms, had nothing to give a poor beggar
at her door—nothing but *Minne*. Adopting for the moment the language
of an aristocratic chatelaine, she graciously offers this one gift to the
mendicant, out of pity. The speech is apparently intended to provoke a
smile—but it is also a commentary on the husband's treatment of wife
and home as if they were goods in a shop.[9] Of this wife too it might be
said that "pitee renneth soone in gentil herte"—except that she belongs
to the wrong estate. The situation is the reverse in the *Merchant's Tale*.
Here members of the highest estate, the aristocracy, are presented to us
in conventional relationship to one another. But instead of romance, the
traditional and appropriate plot for such people, we find them enacting
a *fabliau*, the very antithesis of romance. Herein lies the wellspring of
the satire, the cynicism, the implied criticism of all the ideals elsewhere
presented quite seriously as an adjunct of chivalry. To my way of thinking
this criticism is one of the most dazzling proofs of Chaucer's humane
genius. A bitter admixture of vulgar cynicism derived from the *fabliaux*
was the antidote which would inevitably be tried by a spirit large enough
to rise above the traditional barriers and forms in treating courtly love.
It is not the mere fact of Chaucer's savagery towards unlovely people
which endears him to us (to use Professor Tatlock's expression)—but the
awareness that there is a fundamental falsity in the system, which can
be most clearly revealed, in this case, by a juxtaposition of romance and
fabliaux.

The significance of the *Merchant's Tale* arises in part, then, from its
place in the general trend of Chaucer's attitude to the code of love. It
should not be regarded as an isolated composition, despite its technical

---

[9] F. H. von der Hagen, *Gesammtabenteur*. 2. 245–48.

skill and variety of appeal. The point of view towards which Chaucer was developing is enunciated with simply clarity in the *Manciple's Tale:* /211/

H 212

> Ther nys no difference, trewely,
> Bitwixe a wyf that is of heigh degree,
> If of hir body dishonest she bee,
> And a povre wenche, oother than this—
> If it so be they werke bothe amys—
> But that the *gentile, in estaat above,*
> She shal be cleped his lady, as in love;
> And for that oother is a povre womman,
> She shal be cleped his wenche or his lemman.
> And, God it woot, myn owene deere brother,
> Men leyn that oon as lowe as lith that oother.

This strikes at the very roots of the system as expounded by Andreas. It denies the difference between a *Rusticana Mulier* and a high court lady "if so it be they werke bothe amys"; it denies the importance of "estate" (or class) in judging of these matters. It is the negation of the standards accepted unquestionably by the Dreamer in the *Romance of the Rose.* A "povre wenche" of the country, as Andreas had said, is to be sought *violento amplexu,* without waste of time. A lady is to be wooed by intricate and long deferred advances. But the real distinction is one of "estaat."

There are other reasons than the social ones for rejecting courtly love. The conflict of its standards with religion was also apparent to Chaucer. Nowhere does he rise to a greater height than in the delineation of that spiritual vision which, coming to Troilus after death, causes him to reject with incredulity and divine laughter the very springs of action, the aristocratic emotions and aspirations, which had caused him such real agony when he still dwelt on "this litel spot of erthe, that with the se Embraced is." The sudden and exalted shift in his sense of proportion has the impact of a divine release of comedy.

V 1821

> And in hymself he lough right at the wo
> Of hem that wepten for his deth so faste;
> And dampned al oure werk that folweth so
> The blynde lust, the which that may not laste.

On a much humbler plane we can sense something of the like commentary in the very cynicism and obscenity of the *Merchant's Tale.* Here we are reminded, not of the splendors of the universe and its nine concentric spheres as contrast for the petty preoccupations of *l'amour courtois,* but of the similar /212/ goal desired by chivalrous lover and village seducer alike. The machinery of romance, so apt for concealment of this similar-

ity, is introduced in all its traditional forms. If it were any other than
the mature Chaucer speaking, we might sit back, secure in our fore-
knowledge of the type of play to be enacted. But the plot is given an un-
expected twist, and behold, we find ourselves mocking Damian where he
had suffered fraternally with Troilus. More mildly we feel the same ludicrous incongruity in the *Nun's Priest's Tale*, where the formulas of courtly
love are burlesqued in another way: by introduction into the barnyard;
the cock is described in terms applicable to a knight, and is even compared remotely to Lancelot; the hen insists on the chivalric virtues (even
secrecy!) from her spouse, and yet the pretensions are doubly laughable
because they are associated with that agricultural labor which, according
to Andreas, is completely alien to the practice of love.

Chaucer's was by no means a reforming spirit. It must not be assumed
from any of this that he refused to accept the division of society into
estates, or that he had any sympathy with

The murmure and the cherles rebellyng

which so startled England in his lifetime. His satire of courtly love because of its limitation to a certain class led him to no revolutionary con-
clusions, whether political or other. But he was too keen an observer of
men and morals not to perceive one of the most significant reasons for
the absurdity of its pretensions. The *Merchant's Tale*, with its burlesque
of plots like the *Amadas et Ydoine*, and its deliberate combination of
romance with *fabliau*, shows the clarity of his perception. One source of
its significance is its relation to the general course of his intellectual development. That he achieved the detachment from his *milieu* which enabled him to write the lines quoted from the *Manciple's Tale* is I think a
sign of his peculiar genius. The *Merchant's Tale*, indicative of the same
detachment in another manner, is the more precious to us because of the
very qualities which have in the past led some critics to ignore it out of
personal distaste or to condemn it because they missed the very essence
of its satire.

J. A. Burrow

Irony in the Merchant's Tale*

The *Merchant's Tale* is usually classed as a 'fabliau tale', and the classification has its point. But it has perhaps drawn attention away from those qualities which distinguish the *Merchant's Tale* from the rest of Chaucer's 'fabliaux'. These are qualities which it shares, not with the comic tales of the Miller or the Summoner, but with the moral fable of the Pardoner—the persistent irony, the seriousness which informs even the farcical climax. This climax (the gulling of January in the 'pear-tree episode') is no more simply comic than the death of the Pardoner's rioters. It is much more closely realised than, for example, the dénouement of the *Miller's Tale*; and Chaucer, in filling out the fabliau form in this way, makes something new. The French fabliaux may be cruel, but they are also casual—one gets just enough about, for example, the duped husband to make the joke, and no more. The comic effect depends on the preservation of the skeletal bareness of the story. The reader is never allowed to get near enough, as it were, to be seriously involved. In contrast, the *Merchant's Tale* is full of 'close-ups':

> ... Januarie hath faste in armes take
> His fresshe May, his paradys, his make.
> He lulleth hire, he kisseth hire ful ofte,
> With thikke brustles of his berd unsofte,
> Lyk to the skyn of houndfyssh, sharp as brere,
> For he was shave al newe in his manere.   (E. 1821–1826)

The clarity of the observation is given a sharp point, here, by the simile of the dogfish, and by the ironic comment in the last line. The reader is forced to visualise the scene, as never in the French fabliau, to grasp its

* Reprinted from *Anglia*, LXXV, No. 2 (1957), 199–208, by permission of the author and the publisher.

human reality; and in the process the moral issues, with which the French
authors were not concerned (Bédier called them 'amoral'), come alive.
/200/

Unlike the other 'fabliau tales', but like the *Pardoner's Tale*, the story
of January and May faces up to the moral issues it raises. This involves a
radical modification of the fabliau method. The treatment of January's
dream life (his 'fantasye') recalls, not the carpenter or the miller, but the
Pardoner's rioters with their dreams of wealth:

> This yongeste which that wente to the toun
> Ful ofte in herte he rolleth up and doun
> The beautee of thise floryns newe and brighte.   (C. 837–9)

> Heigh fantasye and curious bisynesse
> Fro day to day gan in the soule impresse
> Of Januarie aboute his mariage.
> Many fair shap and many a fair visage
> Ther passeth thurgh his herte nyght by nyght.   (E. 1577–81)

But it is the distinguishing characteristic of the *Merchant's Tale* that the
ironic contrast between the dream and the reality, the self-centred and
insecure 'heigh fantasye' of the old knight and the predictable course of
his marriage, should be pointed insistently at every turn. In the *Pardoner's
Tale* there is a strong general dramatic irony. The rioters pursue their
own downfall; and they ignore the old man, as January ignores Justinus.
But there is nothing like the accumulation of local irony which marks
the *Merchant's Tale*.

Take, for example, the opening passage of the poem (lines 1245–1398)
where January, in what is really an internal monologue, persuades himself that he will find permanent 'ioye and blisse' in marriage with a young
wife. The general irony of this is clear. The mistake would have been as
obvious to a medieval reader as the rioters' mistake about the gold ('But
mighte this gold be caried from this place . . . than were we in heigh
felicitee'). But the point is made more heavily—January's dotage is much
more ridiculous than anything in the *Pardoner's Tale*. He turns proverbial and biblical lore inside out in a way that places him decisively in the
moral scheme of the poem—'Old fissh and yong flessh wolde I have ful
fayn', 'Do alwey so as wommen wol thee rede'. These lines, and lines like
them, suggest the proverbs of which they are distortions (elsewhere in
Chaucer—'Wommenes conseils been ful ofte colde' 'Men /201/ sholde
wedden after hir estaat, For youthe and elde is often at debaat'). One
more quotation will illustrate the tone of the poem's opening:

> Alle othere manere yiftes hardily
> As londes, rentes, pasture or commune,
> Or moebles, alle been yiftes of fortune,

That passen as a shadwe upon a wal.
But drede nat, if pleynly speke I shal,
A wyf wol laste, and in thyn hous endure,
Wel lenger than thee list, paraventure. (E. 1312–18)

The last line makes a joke out of what is obviously a philosophical
blunder. It is interpolated into the sequence of January's thoughts to
point the irony, like an aside in an Elizabethan play. January is subjected
to the most unblinking scrutiny throughout the poem. His fantastic
thoughts and desires, his slack skin and his bristles, are all rendered in
unsparing detail; and every detail carries a point, strengthening the general with a local irony:

Adoun by olde Januarie she lay
That sleep til that the coughe hath him awaked.   (E. 1956–57)

(This technique is familiar from the General Prologue, where the poetry
is all detail—of behaviour or dress or appearance—and the ironies depend
on the implications of the details). The insistent irony, and the answering
choice of detail, expose the characters of the poem in a brilliant light,
which makes the *Pardoner's Tale* feel almost kindly by comparison.

Now, although Chaucer was by no means always 'gentle Chaucer', he
was not characteristically a destructive poet. His irony, as in the portrait
of the Prioress, is often so fleeting as to be genuinely ambiguous, at least
to the modern reader; his tone is most often that of Theseus in the
Knight's Tale—'The god of love, a benedicite, How mighty and how greet
a lord is he'—and can modulate easily, as in the same speech of Theseus,
into a sympathetic generalization—'A man moot be a fool, or yong or
oold, I woot it by myself ful yore agon'. It is an irony which does justice
to its vicitms; the destructive or critical impulse does not work unchecked.
Of course, there is no *a priori* reason why *Merchant's Tale* should not be
an exception to this /202/ generalization; it might be argued that a ruthless almost hysterical story was called for at this point in the 'Marriage
Group' from the disillusioned Merchant. But I want to suggest that the
'corrosive, destructive, even hopeless quality' which Mr. Patch, and other
critics, found in this poem, and with which I have so far been concerned,
is not the whole story; and that, if it were, the poem would not be as
good as it is. The *Merchant's Tale* is not only a poem of clarity, critical
observation, and disgust—a medieval *Madame Bovary*. There is an opposing impulse, an impulse to approach and understand, which appears
in a tendency to *generalize*. This I consider to be a feature of all Chaucer's
best narrative poetry.

Take one line from the description of January's marriage—'tendre
youthe hath wedded stouping age'. The point is a critical one again (it

is the old fish and young flesh theme) but there is no mistaking the
genuine lyrical note. There is generalization, but it is not the dry generalization of a proverb inside out. A generosity about the line contrasts
sharply with the nagging irony we have been noting. The gentle contrast
between 'stouping' and 'tendre' is not like the sharp and disgusting physical contrast between January's bristly chin and May's 'tendre face' in the
description of the wedding night from which a passage has already been
quoted. There is a generous lyrical note about the line which we find
again in the introduction of Bacchus and Venus into the wedding fes-
tivities:

> Bacus the wyn hem skynketh al aboute,
> And Venus laugheth upon every wight,
> For Januarie was bicome hir knyght,
> And wolde bothe assayen his corage
> In libertee and eek in mariage;
> And with hire fyrbrond in hire hand aboute
> Daunceth biforn the bryde and all the route.   (E. 1722–8)

There is malice in the equating of liberty with marriage; but hardly, it
seems, any mock heroic effect in the introduction of Bacchus and Venus.
January's marriage takes on a festal dignity in the archaic 'skynketh', and
the last buoyant couplet. There is another finer couplet on this theme a
little later:

> So sore hath Venus hurt hym with hire brond
> As that she bar it daunsing in hire hond./203/   (E. 1777–8)

(Here the 'daunsing' can refer either to Venus, or to the torch; it effectively goes with both). The effect of such lines as these is to dignify the
emotions involved by setting them in the general context of human feelings represented by the gods. It will be clear from these examples that
there is nothing thin or abstract about the generalization. It is done concretely, and is felt as a sort of lyrical expansiveness in the verse (an effect
I do not find in the *Pardoner's Tale*).

There is, further, a perceptible drift towards allegory in the poem. The
names January and May, Justinus and Placebo, suggest this. At one point
there is a significant reference to what for Chaucer was the allegory par
excellence, the *Romance of the Rose*:

> He made a gardyn, walled al with stoon,
> So fair a gardyn woot I nowher noon.
> For, out of doute, I verraily suppose
> That he that wroot the Romance of the Rose
> Ne coude of it the beautee wel devyse . . .   (E. 2029–33)

The garden, which is here being introduced, plays an important part in the poem. As it serves to dignify and strengthen January's feelings by generalizing them, and to counter the 'corrosive' irony to which they are exposed, it may fittingly be considered here.

January's desire for a young wife is presented from the start as 'fantasye' —self deception (the word is a favourite of Chaucer's, occuring very frequently in *Troilus and Criseyde*). But it is associated equally, in a series of contexts as the beginning of the poem, with the image of the earthly paradise, the general fantasy of the great good place. 'Wedlock' January thinks 'is so esy and so clene That in this world it is a paradys' . . . 'Wyf is mannes help and his confort His paradys terrestre and his desport'. Then at the wedding 'Januarie hath faste in armes take His fresshe May, his paradys, his make'. Marriage is like the earthly paradise quite specifically in being at once 'esy' and 'clene'—delightful and morally irreproachable. Desire and duty are at one in marriage, as January points out to May on their wedding night—'Blessed be the yok that we be inne For in our actes we mowe do no sinne'. /204/

It is true that January's 'heigh fantasye' is made to look ridiculous in the poem. When he worries lest he should have 'myn hevene in erthe here' and pay for it later, Justinus remarks:

> Dispeire yow noght, but have in youre memorie,
> Peraunter she may be youre purgatorie.
> She may be Goddes mene, and Goddes whippe,
> Thanne shal youre soule up to hevene skippe
> Swifter than dooth an arwe out of a bowe.   (E. 1669–73)

But it is not only ridiculous. It draws strength from association with the image of the earthly paradise (or the garden of Genesis as is clear from lines 1325–32). January's 'fantasye' is broadened by these allusions to include a general human fantasy; it is not only the delusion of a besotted *senex amans*. Here again the generalizing lends dignity and significance to the action of the poem, contributing to the reader's sense of an intelligible and meaningful narrative progression.

It seems clear that in this progression January's garden in the second part of the poem takes over from the image of the 'paradys terrestre' in the first. It is in fact the paradys of his sexual fantasy realised; in the poem the garden has something approaching a symbolic status (as gardens often have in medieval literature). The opening of the description has already been quoted. It goes on:

> Ne Priapus ne myghte nat suffise,
> Though he be god of gardyns, for to telle

> The beautee of the gardyn and the welle
> That stood under a laurer alwey grene.   (E. 2034–7)

The *Romance of the Rose* has already been explicitly introduced into the description, and the well under the laurel is certainly meant to recall the well in the garden of the *Romance* which, in Chaucer's translation, lies 'under a tree, Which tree in Fraunce men cal a pyn'. The laurel must have been substituted for the pine to link the garden with January's erotic fantasies. It is meant to recall his earlier boast:

> Though I be hoor, I fare as dooth a tree
> That blosmeth er the fruyt ywoxen bee;
> And blosmy tree nys neither drye ne deed./205/
> I feele me nowhere hoor but on myn heed;
> Myn herte and alle my lymes been as grene
> As laurer thurgh the yeer is for to sene.   (E. 1461–6)

This suggests that Chaucer is considering more than the narrative necessities in organising the detail of the tale. There is a further suggestion of the sexual significance of the garden in the introduction of Priapus here. The repetition, through the opening description (2029–37), of the words 'garden' and 'beauty' gives to the lines an emphatic, almost incantatory, ring, which disposes the reader to look for 'meanings', as if it were the garden of the *Parlement* or of Dante's *Purgatorio*. It is in this garden of love, for such it clearly seems to be, that January 'payes his wyf hir dette'. He guards it as jealously as if it were May herself, and walls it off, like the garden of Guillaume Lorris, with stone.

January goes blind, and the extravagance of his jealousy (it is 'outrageous') is noted in the best fabliau manner— although not without gestures of sympathy ('O Januarie, what myghte it thee availle Thogh thou myghte se as fer as shippes saille?'). His fantasy, no longer associated with the solid and persuasive ideal image of the fertile garden of love, becomes almost imbecile ('He nolde suffre hir for to ryde or go. But if that he had hand on hire alwey'). But, with the opening of the final scene in the garden, the tone changes again:

> . . . in a morwe unto this May seith he:
> 'Rys up, my wyf, my love, my lady free,
> The turtles voys is herd, my dowve sweete,
> The wynter is goon with alle his reynes weete.
> Com forth now with thyne eyen columbyn,
> How fairer been thy brestes than is wyn.
> The gardyn is enclosed al aboute.
> Com forth my white spouse! . .   (E. 2137–44)

This very striking passage, as Skeat pointed out, is a mosaic of phrases from the *Song of Solomon*. It is beautifully timed. The strong impersonal

lyric note re-establishes January's passion, bringing out the essential in-
telligibility of his behaviour, making sense of him again after the fabliau
comedy of the preceding passage. And the garden, the symbolic home of
his /206/ ideal of fertility and privacy, gains a further reference. 'The
gardyn is enclosed al aboute' recalls, from the *Song of Solomon*: 'A garden
enclosed is my sister, my spouse; a spring shut up, a fountain sealed'.
Chaucer has turned this metaphor into a literal statement about January's
walled garden, and it might seem that the resulting line would sit oddly
in the middle of the passage, which in general preserves the elaborately
metaphoric style of the biblical original. That it seems quite natural suggests how the literal garden of Chaucer's poem has itself gathered a kind
of metaphorical significance.

This is not to deny that there is meant to be some kind of mock-heroic
effect in the passage, although I think it is faint. The passage primarily
works in the other direction, resisting the 'corrosive' irony. Chaucer certainly damps the Solomon passage down with his comment 'Swiche olde
lewed wordes used he' (where 'lewed' seems to mean 'lecherous' rather
than 'ignorant'). But the final effect is rather of pathos than of irony. As
January speaks, Damyan slips in through the gate and hides behind a
bush; and January, 'blynd as is a stoon', follows him in with May. He *is*
presented as pathetic, absurd, and repulsive (there is more pathos in him
as the poem progresses, though this never involves any sort of moral con-
cession towards him on the author's part). But he is not only the object
of ironic sympathy and contempt. Chaucer makes out of his sexual 'fantasye' something that the reader can feel is real and intelligible, by ex-
tending the poem's field of reference beyond the range of its narrative
particularities, drawing on the common literary experience of his culture.
The *Romance of the Rose* and the Bible were the obvious common points
of reference (knowledge of the Italian poets was much more restricted),
and these works are very much present in the *Merchant's Tale*.

This width of reference seems to me to be a general characteristic of
Chaucer's best poetry. It is this which marks the *Merchant's Tale* off from
the two other fabliau tales which are sometimes associated with it—the
Friar's Tale and the *Summoner's Tale*. These poems have in common with
the *Merchant's Tale* a quality of destructive wit (which appears at its
best in the ironically observed speeches of the Friar to /207/ Thomas)
and of farcical popular humour (which appears in the dénouements of
the poems). The anecdotes are filled out with ironic detail. The Friar
comes to see Thomas:

> . . . fro the bench he droof awey the cat,
> And leyde adoun his potente and his hat,
> And eek his scrippe, and sette hym softe adoun.   (D. 1775–7)

The Friar's smooth impudence is superbly conveyed in the rhythm and even the rhyme of these lines. It is comedy—more obviously comedy than the close-up of January sitting up in bed which was quoted earlier. The first part of the *Summoner's Tale* is brilliantly successful. But if we compare the poem as a whole with the *Merchant's Tale* we may feel that it lacks solidity. The Friar is taken at his face value—the common satiric type of the corrupt cleric. The tone of the poem never modulates from the ironic and critical; the method is exclusively mimetic. It is 'poetry of the surface'. We find these qualities in the *Merchant's Tale* too. But January's behaviour is not only observed, it is explored (the key word, I have suggested, is 'fantasye'). It is traced back to a compelling sexual fantasy, which is linked, through the garden, with the fantasies of the Earthly Paradise, the *Song of Songs*, and the *Romance of the Rose*. There is a lyrical expansiveness ('tendre youthe hath wedded stoupyng age') in the poem, where the anecdote is being generalized in this way. The particularity of the *Summoner's Tale* is invigorating (at least in the earlier part) ; but in the end the poem does not add up to much. It remains an extended anecdote.

It seems obvious that the quality of the *Merchant's Tale* which is being described bears some relation to Allegory. The allegorical suggestions of the names January and May, Placebo and Justinus, are apparent enough. The reader of *Piers Plowman* will recognise in the system of cross-references which links January's garden with other gardens, and all these gardens with the theme of sexual fantasy, a familiar technique. It bears little relation to the strict allegorical method, which some critics detect in *Piers*—the method of four-level meaning deriving, ultimately, from biblical interpretation; but neither does most medieval allegory. Usually the technique is loose, /208/ flexible, and intermittent. The equations may for a time be very fixed and clear ('Petrus id est Christus') ; but they may equally well amount to nothing more than a casual cross-reference. Only on a too rigid definition could the part played by the allegorical method in the *Merchant's Tale* be ignored. Its story is not in itself allegorical; neither is the story of the Eighteenth Passus of *Piers Plowman* (the story of the crucifixion and resurrection) with which, technically, the poem has something in common. In both, allegory is at work generalising and equating (Christ is Light is Piers; January is Age, his garden is Adam's and Solomon's and Lorris'). In both, allegorical figures can enter the story without anomaly (Mercy, Peace, Truth and Righteousness; Venus and Bacchus).

The point here is that this generalizing impulse (characteristic of allegory) exists side by side in Chaucer with the ironic or satiric impulse (characteristic of fabliau), which tends to isolate its object and particularize it. It is this dual impulse which makes the *Merchant's Tale* a saner and more balanced poem than the conventional account might suggest. It is unlike the *Summoner's Tale* in having a significance beyond its anecdotal content, in having a 'meaning'. The irony is controlled (and this is surely characteristic of Chaucer) by a recognition that January's case illustrates general human weakness—a suggestion that is rigidly excluded in the treatment of the Summoner's Friar. It is a knowledge of 'fantasye' which informs the poem and gives it its moral framework within which the irony works. This knowledge appears in the unobtrusively allegorical treatment of the story, notably of the garden. The poem owes as much to the allegory as to the fabliau, bringing to the anecdotal clarity of the latter a scope and significance which belong to the former tradition. This seems to be one of the secrets of Chaucer's best narrative poems. They grow in the mind without losing the precision of their outline.

Robert J. Blanch

Irony in Chaucer's
*Merchant's Tale**

The *Merchant's Tale* contains three major categories of irony—verbal, rhetorical, and dramatic. Verbal irony, wherein the literal expression is the opposite of the intended meaning, may be found in the Merchant's introductory comments upon marriage and in his use of *double entendre*. Rhetorical, on the other hand, reveals an inverse treatment of courtly love traditions and is expressed by the employment of exaggerated figures of speech for the purpose of subsequent deflation. Finally, dramatic irony is "the irony resulting from a strong contrast, unperceived by a character in a story, between the surface meaning of his words or deeds and something else happening in the same story."[1]

Verbal irony is disclosed both directly, through the Merchant's lavish praise, and indirectly, through his equivocal remarks. In his panegyric on marriage, the Merchant pretends to cherish the pious aspirations and foolish optimisms which flit through January's mind. However, as revealed by the Prologue to the *Merchant's Tale*, the Merchant's marriage "Thise monthes two" to a "shrewe" has embittered him. Although the Merchant does not allude explicitly to his hellish marriage, his personal experience colors the tale. With his grandiloquence masking his savage sneer, the Merchant utters noble words about marriage, really ironic curses "extorted by the spectacle of an amorous fool whom he is about to expose."[2] For example, the Merchant lavishly praises the merits of a good wife while loathing her: /9/

> If he be povre, she helpeth hym to swynke;
> She kepeth his good, and wasteth never a deel;

---

* Reprinted from *The Lock Haven Review*, VIII (1966), 8–15, by permission of the editor.

[1] Germaine Dempster, *Dramatic Irony in Chaucer* (New York, 1959), p. 251.

[2] G. G. Sedgewick, "The Structure of the *Merchant's Tale*," *The University of Toronto Quarterly*, XVII (July, 1948), 342.

> Al that hire housbonde lust, hire liketh weel;
> She seith nat ones "Nay," whan he seith "ye."
> "Do this," seith he; "Al redy, sire," seith she.[3]

In the midst of his exaggerated praise, the Merchant sprinkles several equivocal remarks. He notes that "A wyf wol laste, and in thyn hous endure, / Wel lenger than thee list, paraventure" (E, 1317–18) and that "They [husband and wife] been so knit ther may noon harm bitide, / And namely upon the wives side" (E, 1391–92). In each instance, the words seem to puncture the mask assumed by the Merchant. Perhaps, these words also enable the Merchant to poke fun at January's self-deception and naïveté since only a naïve individual could overlook such remarks.

Furthermore, the Merchant employs puns or *double entendres* in his tale. Unscrupulous May, the embodiment of vernal fertility and sexual energy, is called "fresshe May" the moment Damian begins to desire her; henceforth, "fresshe" is repeated so often that it becomes a fixed epithet.[4] Later on, in the pear-tree episode, Pluto affirms that he will restore January's sight the moment Damian and May cuckold him. Pluto alludes to Damian as "the lechour, in the tree!" (E, 2257), but Proserpina, who furnishes May with an excuse for her act when she and Damian are discovered, views the act differently. It becomes the panacea for January's blindness. "The 'lecher' Damian becomes a 'healer' or 'doctor' (from ME *lecher*)."[5] Ironically, the "doctor-healer" is named after one of the two patron saints of physicians—St. Damian.[6] /10/

Also, in the pear-tree episode, it is noted that January ". . . saugh that Damyan his wyf had dressed / In swich manere it may nat been expressed" (E, 2361–62). The word 'dressed' may be construed as 'arrayed' or 'addressed'.[7]

All of these elements, woven together into the fabric of meaning underlying the *Merchant's Tale*, constitute verbal irony. A second type of irony, albeit a significant one, emanates from Chaucer's singular use of rhetorical techniques.

In the hands of Chaucer, exaggerated classical references are employed to underscore the Merchant's ironic attitude toward January. At the marriage feast, for example, the high-flown rhetoric seems inappropriate:

> Biforn hem stoode instrumentz of swiche soun
> That Orpheus, ne of Thebes Amphioun,

---

[3] F. N. Robinson (ed.), *The Works of Geoffrey Chaucer* (Boston, 1957), E, ll. 1342–1346, Subsequent quotations will have their line references in parentheses.

[4] Paul F. Baum, "Chaucer's Puns," *PMLA*, LXXI (March, 1956), p. 239.

[5] Philip M. Griffith, "Chaucer's *Merchant's Tale*," *Explicator*, XVI (December, 1957), #13.

[6] *Ibid.*

[7] Baum, *op. cit.*, p. 237.

> Ne maden nevere swich a melodye.
> At every cours thanne cam loud mynstralcye,
> That nevere tromped Joab for to heere,
> Nor he Theodomas, yet half so cleere,
> At Thebes, whan the citee was in doute.
> Bacus the wyn her shynketh al aboute,
> And Venus laugheth upon every wight,
> For Januarie was bicome hir knyght   (E, 1715–24).

Similarly, poetic language seems ill-placed prior to the description of Pluto, the King of "fairye," and his queen, Proserpina. The sweet setting is in opposition to the ugly reality of May's adulterous relationship with Damian:

> Bright was the day, and blew the firmament;
> Phebus hath of gold his stremes doun ysent,
> To gladen every flour with his warmnesse.
> He was that tyme in Geminis, as I gesse,
> But litel fro his declynacion
> Of Cancer, Jovis exaltacion   (E, 2219–2224).

In each instance, however, exaggerated classical allusions and rhetoric are employed by the Merchant to depict January's /ll/ dependence upon a dream world of "fantasye." The marriage feast represents the culmination of January's misconceptions of marital "ese" and "blisse." On the other hand, the Merchant's introduction to the Pluto-Proserpina description is apropos because Pluto, the King of "fairye," is the mythological counterpart of January, the victim of "fairye" and "fantasye." Any hyperbolic rhetoric, then, would emphasize January's inflated egotism and delusion.

Likewise, the Merchant's use of apostrophes and heroic similes, the trappings of the courtly love tradition, indicates an ironic purpose—to build up what he despises. In one instance, the Merchant feigns concern over Damian's perfidious conduct:

> O perilous fyr, that in the bedstraw bredeth!
> O famulier foo, that his servyce bedeth!
> O servant traytour, false hoomly hewe,
> Lyk to the naddre in bosom sly untrewe   (E, 1783–86).

Rhetorical irony is also manifested by the Merchant's inverse treatment of courtly love traditions.[8] Although she is married to January, May flings aside all moral considerations and announces that she loves Damian "best of any creature" (E, 1984). Against this statement of duplicity the Merchant juxtaposes a theme of the courtly love tradition—"Lo, pitee renneth

---

8 Sedgewick, *op. cit.*, p. 342.

soone in gentil herte!" (E, 1986). Even though it is obvious that the Merchant does not really mean to ascribe any tenderness to May, the ironic implications of courtly love phraseology are expanded when May insists she is "a gentil womman and no wenche" (E, 2202).

Part of the courtly love tradition—genteel language—is used to avert lascivious desires. In speaking of the union between a husband and wife, the Merchant affirms that "The blisse which that is bitwixe hem tweye / Ther may no tonge telle, or herte thynk" (E, 1340–41). Similarly, when the Merchant alludes to sexual intercourse between Damian and May, he notes that January ". . . saugh that Damyan his wyf had dressed / In swich manere it may nat been expressed" (E, 2361–62). /12/

The Merchant's employment of genteel language, an affected nicety, represents ironically his attempt to cloak the theme of adultery which pervades the tale. Even the "courtly" love of Damian and May is described in a mechanical way because it is precipitated by sensuality—thus achieving an ironic effect.[9]

The final category under consideration is dramatic irony, an irony which postulates a deeper understanding of the character's spoken word or action based upon the superior knowledge of the audience. The first significant examples of dramatic irony are found in January's allusions to the paradisaical nature of marriage: ". . . wedlock is so esy and so clene, / That in this world it is a paradys" (E, 1264–65) and ". . . wyf is mannes helpe and his confort, /His paradys terrestre, and his disport" (E, 1331–32). Marriage is analogous to an earthly paradise because it is joyful and morally irreproachable.[10] However, in linking marriage with an Edenic state, January does not perceive the full import of his words. Every paradise, no matter how idyllic, will be vitiated by sin, thus anticipating adultery in the pear-tree episode.

Following his panegyric on marriage, January apotheosizes several Biblical women:

> Lo, how that Jacob, as thise clerkes rede,
> By good conseil of his mooder Rebekke,
> Boond the kydes skyn aboute his nekke,
> For which his fadres benyson he wan.
> Lo Judith, as the storie eke telle kan,
> By wys conseil she Goddes peple kepte,
> And slow hym Olofernus, whil he slepte.
> Lo Abigayl, by good conseil, how she
> Saved hir housbonde Nabal, whan that he
> Sholde han be slayn   (E, 1362–1371).

[9] Charles Muscatine, *Chaucer and the French Tradition* (Los Angeles, 1957), p. 231.
[10] J. A. Burrow, "Irony in the *Merchant's Tale*," *Anglia*, LXXV (1957), p. 200.

Ironically, January's dotage is emphasized by these Biblical allusions because every example involves a woman whose "conseil" /13/ is associated with deceit. While attempting to uphold the integrity of women by establishing Biblical models, January unwittingly destroys his argument, for the wiles of the Old Testament heroines adumbrate the deception employed by May.

Similarly, January's imperceptiveness is illustrated by his initial conversation with "his bretheren two", Justinus and Placebo. January stubbornly resolves, spurred on by lust and desire for salvation, to marry a young woman because ". . . a yong thyng may men gye, / Right as men may warm wex with handes plye" (E, 1429–30). Although January believes that May's nature is as pliant as warm wax, he cannot know that May will later employ this substance to counterfeit a key, thus permitting Damian to enter January's garden.[11] January then explains to his friends that he is the final judge of a marriage partner although "Ther speketh many a man of mariage / That woot namoore of it than woot my page" (E, 1443–44). January's statement dramatically foreshadows Damian's future relationship with May, wherein Damian, one of January's followers, will be initiated into the sexual mysteries of marriage.

After January decides to marry May, he is fearful lest he should lose his chance of heavenly bliss because of his enjoyment of a "paradys terrestre".[12] Not being clairvoyant enough to perceive the future adulterous relationship between Damian and May, January notes the "parfit felicitee" of marriage and worries about not having his share of earthly ". . . tribulacion and greet penaunce" (E, 1649). Justinus, however, reassures January by inserting a skillful ironic note: "Dispeire yow noght, but have in youre memorie, / Paraunter she may be youre purgatorie!" (E, 1669–70).

Following his conversation with Justinus, January—complacent and triumphant—prepares for his marriage to May. May is enjoined to ". . . be lyk Sarra and Rebekke / In wysdom /14/ and in trouthe of mariage" (E, 1704–05), thereby anticipating May's future rejection of marital virtues.[13] The marriage service concludes when the priest ". . . made al siker ynogh with hoolynesse" (E, 1708). It is thus clear that the marriage ceremony is inefficacious because it does not ensure a permanent, holy union between January and May. May will soon defile the sacrament of marriage through her extramarital affair with Damian.

When the wedding ceremony is completed, January and May attend a

---

[11] J. S. P. Tatlock, "Chaucer's *Merchant's Tale*," *Modern Philology*, XXXIII (May, 1936), p. 373.

[12] Dempster, *op. cit.*, p. 53.

[13] J. S. P. Tatlock, "The Marriage Service in Chaucer's *Merchant's Tale*," *Modern Language Notes*, XXXII (June, 1917), pp. 373–374.

feast. As the hours wear on, January becomes impatient and prays to God ". . . that it were woxen nyght, / And that the nyght wolde lasten everemo" (E, 1762–63). January's wish is fulfilled, for his spiritual blindness ('nyght'), precipitated by egotism, sensuality, and delusion, is not ephemeral. After the guests leave the wedding feast, January ". . . Kisseth hire [May] ful ofte; / With thikke brustles of his berd unsofte, / Lyk to the skyn of houndfyssh, sharp as brere— / For he was shave al newe in his manere-" (E, 1823–26). This grotesque portrait of January's bristly skin contrasts sharply with May's "tendre face" and emphasizes January's unawareness of himself, of May, and of the impression he produces.

With his sexual appetite satisfied, January soon learns that Damian is ill, actually love-sick for May. Feeling compassion for Damian, January orders May to visit him, thereby enabling Damian to give May the letter professing his love for her. Shortly afterwards, January, the future dupe, ". . . made a gardyn, walled al with stoon" (E, 2029), the setting for adultery and his undoing.[14] However, January's happiness with May in his garden is shattered when he becomes blind, the physical counterpart of his spiritual blindness.

At this point, January becomes a major target of deception. Even the allusion to the *Song of Solomon*—"No spot of thee ne knew I al my lyf" (E, 2146)—further emphasizes his de- /15/ ception. The irony inherent in the contrast between January's passion and the sacred association of the *Song of Solomon* equals the irony of his being as unconscious of the physical spot which he now touches as he will later be of the moral blot, adultery, when he views it with unblinded eyes.[15]

The final examples of dramatic irony are found in the concluding scene of the *Merchant's Tale*. With his arms embracing the trunk of the pear tree, January helps May to engage in adultery. Even when January's sight is restored and he actually sees May copulating with Damian, May convinces January that what he sees is an optical illusion. After May "leep doun fro the tree" (E, 2411), January strokes her womb caressingly, the womb conventionally being described as the shape of an inverted pear.

Although employed to ridicule self-deception and to desentimentalize marriage, it should be noted from the examples above that, collectively, the three categories of irony constitutes Chaucer's most effective device for projecting a basic conflict between "fantasye" and reality.

---

[14] Dempster, *op. cit.*, p. 56.

[15] Charles A. Owen, Jr., "The Crucial Passages in Five of the *Canterbury Tales*: A Study in Irony and Symbol," *Journal of English and Germanic Philology*, LII (July, 1953), p. 299.

Suggestions for Papers

Compare and contrast the views of B. H. Bronson and R. M. Jordan with those of J. S. P. Tatlock, G. G. Sedgewick, and P. A. Olson.

Examine carefully the relationship between the Merchant and the tale he narrates. Is there any real "tension" between the *Merchant's Tale* and its teller?

In what ways does the prologue to the *Merchant's Tale* intensify the irony in the tale itself?

Is the inclusion of Pluto and Proserpine in the *Merchant's Tale* a typical literary use of *deus ex machina,* or does the appearance of these two characters add to the organic unity of the *Merchant's Tale?*

Justify (or attack) the poem's mixture of allegorical and ironic elements.

Is the essential tone of the *Merchant's Tale* morally serious or comic?

Compare and contrast the views of marriage expressed in the *Merchant's Tale* and the *Franklin's Tale.*

Compare and contrast Chaucer's use of the garden motif in the *Merchant's Tale* and the *Franklin's Tale.*

Discuss the dependence of both the *Merchant's Tale* and the prologue to the *Wife of Bath's Tale* on medieval antifeminist tracts.

Examine carefully Chaucer's employment of the literary convention of "courtly love" in both the *Merchant's Tale* and the *Franklin's Tale.* Does Chaucer idealize or parody courtly love in these two tales?

Discuss the pear-tree episode in January's garden as a kind of reenactment of the fall of Adam in the Garden of Eden.

Discuss the symbolic implications of the references to blindness in the tale.

Discuss the symbolic implications of the fruit images in the tale.

Explain how Justinus and Placebo represent two sides of January's nature.

In what ways can Pluto be construed as the mythological counterpart of January?

In what ways can Proserpine be construed as the mythological counterpart of May?

What are the chief characteristics of the fabliau? Can the *Merchant's Tale* be termed without qualification a fabliau?

Critically evaluate several interpretations of the *Merchant's Tale* contained in this volume. Which do you prefer? Why?

Discuss Chaucer's use of Biblical allusions in the tale. What thematic purpose do these allusions serve in the tale?

Discuss the relationship between the seasonal connotations of the month of May and the character May in the tale.

Additional Readings

Note: Bibliographies of Chaucer's works include D. D. Griffith, *Bibliography of Chaucer 1908–1953* (Seattle, 1955); William R. Crawford, *Bibilography of Chaucer 1954–63* (Seattle, 1967); and Albert C. Baugh, *Chaucer* (New York, 1968). For an excellent introduction to modern Chaucerian scholarship, see Beryl Rowland, ed., *Companion to Chaucer Studies* (New York, 1968).

Books

Craik, T. W. *The Comic Tales of Chaucer.* London: Methuen and Co., 1964.

Dempster, Germaine. *Dramatic Irony in Chaucer.* New York: Humanities Press, 1959.

Muscatine, Charles. *Chaucer and the French Tradition: A Study in Style and Meaning.* Berkeley and Los Angeles: University of California Press, 1957.

Robertson, D. W., Jr. *A Preface to Chaucer: Studies in Medieval Perspectives.* Princeton: Princeton University Press, 1962.

Ruggiers, Paul G. *The Art of the Canterbury Tales.* Madison: University of Wisconsin Press, 1965.

Articles

Dempster, Germaine. "On the Source of the Deception Story in the *Merchant's Tale*," *Modern Philology*, XXXIV (November, 1936), 133–54.

Economou, George D. "Januarie's Sin against Nature: The *Merchant's Tale* And the *Roman de la Rose*," *Comparative Literature*, XVII (Summer, 1965), 251–57.

Elliott, John R., Jr. "The Two Tellers of *The Merchant's Tale*," *Tennessee Studies in Literature*, IX (1964), 11–17.

Holman, C. Hugh. "Courtly Love in the Merchant's and the Franklin's Tales," *English Literary History*, XVIII (December, 1951), 241–52.

Kaske, R. E. "January's 'Aube'," *Modern Language Notes*, LXXV (January, 1960), 1–4.

Kee, Kenneth. "Two Chaucerian Gardens," *Mediaeval Studies*, XXIII (1961), 154–62.

Kellogg, Alfred L. "Susannah and the *Merchant's Tale*," *Speculum*, XXXV (April, 1960), 275–79.

Loomis, L. H. "Chaucer and the Breton Lays of the Auchinleck MS.," *Studies in Philology*, XXXVIII (January, 1941), 14–33.

McGalliard, John C. "Chaucerian Comedy: The *Merchant's Tale*, Jonson, and Molière," *Philological Quarterly*, XXV (October, 1946), 343–70.

————. "Chaucer's *Merchant's Tale* and Deschamps' *Miroir de Mariage*," *Philological Quarterly*, XXV (July, 1946), 193–220.

Olson, Paul A. "The Merchant's Lombard Knight," *Texas Studies in Literature and Language*, III (1961), 259–63.

Owen, Charles A., Jr. "The Crucial Passages in Five of the *Canterbury Tales*: A Study in Irony and Symbol," *Journal of English and Germanic Philology*, LII (July, 1953), 294–311.

Pittock, Malcolm. "*The Merchant's Tale*," *Essays in Criticism*, XVII (January, 1967), 26–40.

Robertson, D. W., Jr. "The Doctrine of Charity in Mediaeval Literary Gardens: A Topical Approach through Symbolism and Allegory," *Speculum*, XXVI (January, 1951), 24–49.

Wentersdorf, Karl P. "Theme and Structure in *The Merchant's Tale*: The Function of the Pluto Episode," *Publications of the Modern Language Association of America*, LXXX (December, 1965), 522–27.

General Instructions
For A Research Paper

If your instructor gives you any specific directions about the format of your research paper that differ from the directions given here, you are, of course, to follow his directions. Otherwise, you can observe these directions with the confidence that they represent fairly standard conventions.

A research paper represents a student's synthesis of his reading in a number of primary and secondary works, with an indication, in footnotes, of the source of quotations used in the paper or of facts cited in paraphrased material. A *primary* source is the text of a work as it issued from the pen of the author or some document contemporary with the work. The following, for instance, would be considered primary sources: a manuscript copy of the work; first editions of the work and any subsequent editions authorized by the writer; a modern scholarly edition of the text; an author's comment about his work in letters, memoirs, diaries, journals, or periodicals; published comments on the work by the author's contemporaries. A *secondary* source would be any interpretation, explication, or evaluation of the work printed, usually several years after the author's death, in critical articles and books, in literary histories, and in biographies of the author. In this casebook, the text of the work, any variant versions of it, any commentary on the work by the author himself or his contemporaries may be considered as primary sources; the editor's Introduction, the articles from journals, and the excerpts from books are to be considered secondary sources. The paper that you eventually write will become a secondary source.

Plagiarism

The cardinal sin in the academic community is plagiarism. The rankest form of plagiarism is the verbatim reproduction of someone else's words without any indication that the passage is a quotation. A lesser but still serious form of plagiarism is to report, in your own

155

words, the fruits of someone else's research without acknowledging the source of your information or interpretation.

You can take this as an inflexible rule: every verbatim quotation in your paper must be either enclosed in quotation marks or single-spaced and inset from the left-hand margin and must be followed by a footnote number. Students who merely change a few words or phrases in a quotation and present the passage as their own work are still guilty of plagiarism. Passages of genuine paraphrase must be footnoted too if the information or idea or interpretation contained in the paraphrase cannot be presumed to be known by ordinary educated people or at least by readers who would be interested in the subject you are writing about.

The penalties for plagiarism are usually very severe. Don't run the risk of a failing grade on the paper or even of a failing grade in the course.

Lead-Ins

Provide a lead-in for all quotations. Failure to do so results in a serious breakdown in coherence. The lead-in should at least name the person who is being quoted. The ideal lead-in, however, is one that not only names the person but indicates the pertinence of the quotation.

Examples:

> (typical lead-in for a single-spaced, inset quotation)
>
> Irving Babbitt makes this observation about Flaubert's attitude toward women:

(typical lead-in for quotation worked into the frame of one's sentence)

> Thus the poet sets out to show how the present age, as George Anderson puts it, "negates the values of the earlier revolution."[7]

Full Names

The first time you mention anyone in a paper give the full name of the person. Subsequently you may refer to him by his last name.

Examples: First allusion—Ronald S. Crane
Subsequent allusions—Professor Crane, as Crane says.

Ellipses

Lacunae in a direct quotation are indicated with *three spaced periods,* in addition to whatever punctuation mark was in the text at the point where you truncated the quotation. *Hit the space-bar of your type-writer between each period.* Usually there is no need to put the ellipsis-periods at the beginning or the end of a quotation.

Example: "The poets were not striving to communi-
cate with their audience; . . . By and
large, the Romantics were seeking . . .
to express their unique personalities."[8]

Brackets

Brackets are used to enclose any material interpolated into a direct quotation. The abbreviation *sic,* enclosed in brackets, indicates that the error of spelling, grammar, or fact in a direct quotation has been copied as it was in the source being quoted. If your typewriter does not have special keys for brackets, draw the brackets neatly with a pen.

Examples: "He [Theodore Baum] maintained that Con-
fucianism [the primary element in Chinese
philosophy] aimed at teaching each individual to accept his lot in life."[12]

"Paul Revear [sic] made his historic ride
on April 18, 1875 [sic]."[15]

Summary Footnote

A footnote number at the end of a sentence which is not enclosed in quotation marks indicates that only *that* sentence is being docu-mented in the footnote. If you want to indicate that the footnote documents more than one sentence, put a footnote number at the end of the *first* sentence of the paraphrased passage and use some formula like this in the footnote:

[16] For the information presented in this and the
following paragraph, I am indebted to Marvin
Magalaner, Time of Apprenticeship: the Fiction of
Young James Joyce (London, 1959), pp. 81-93.

Citing the Edition

The edition of the author's work being used in a paper should always be cited in the first footnote that documents a quotation from that work. You can obviate the need for subsequent footnotes to that edition by using some formula like this:

⁴ Nathaniel Hawthorne, "Young Goodman Brown," as printed in Young Goodman Brown, ed. Thomas E. Connolly, Charles E. Merrill Literary Casebooks (Columbus, Ohio, 1968), pp. 3-15. This edition will be used throughout the paper, and hereafter all quotations from this book will be documented with a page-number in parentheses at the end of the quotation.

Notetaking

Although all the material you use in your paper may be contained in this casebook, you will find it easier to organize your paper if you work from notes written on 3 x 5 or 4 x 6 cards. Besides, you should get practice in the kind of notetaking you will have to do for other term-papers, when you will have to work from books and articles in, or on loan from, the library.

An ideal note is a self-contained note—one which has all the information you would need if you used anything from that note in your paper. A note will be self-contained if it carries the following information:

(1) The information or quotation *accurately* copied.

(2) Some system for distinguishing direct quotation from para-phrase.

(3) All the bibliographical information necessary for documenting that note—full name of the author, title, volume number (if any), place of publication, publisher, publication date, page numbers.

(4) If a question covered more than one page in the source, the note-card should indicate which part of the quotation occurred on one page and which part occurred on the next page. The easiest way to do this is to put the next page number in parentheses after the last word on one page and before the first word on the next page.

In short, your note should be so complete that you would never have to go back to the original source to gather any piece of information about that note.

Footnote Forms

The footnote forms used here follow the conventions set forth in the *MLA Style Sheet,* Revised Edition, ed. William Riley Parker, which is now used by more than 100 journals and more than thirty university presses in the United States. Copies of this pamphlet can be purchased for fifty cents from your university bookstore or from the Modern Language Association, 62 Fifth Avenue, New York, N.Y. 10011. If your teacher or your institution prescribes a modified form of this footnoting system, you should, of course, follow that system.

A primary footnote, the form used the first time a source is cited, supplies four pieces of information: (1) author's name, (2) title of the source, (3) publication information, (4) specific location in the source of the information or quotation. A secondary footnote is the shorthand form of documentation after the source has been cited in full the first time.

Your instructor may permit you to put all your footnotes on separate pages at the end of your paper. But he may want to give you practice in putting footnotes at the bottom of the page. Whether the footnotes are put at the end of the paper or at the bottom of the page, they should observe this format of spacing: (1) the first line of each footnote should be indented, usually the same number of spaces as your paragraph indentations; (2) all subsequent lines of the footnote should start at the lefthand margin; (3) there should be single-spacing within each footnote and double-spacing between each footnote.

Example:

[10] Ruth Wallerstein, <u>Richard Crashaw</u>: <u>A Study in Style and Poetic Development</u>, University of Wisconsin Studies in Language and Literature, No. 37 (Madison, 1935), p. 52.

Primary Footnotes

(The form to be used the *first* time a work is cited)

[1] Paull F. Baum, <u>Ten Studies in the Poetry of Matthew Arnold</u> (Durham, N.C., 1958), p. 37.

(book by a single author; p. is the abbreviation of *page*)

[2] René Wellek and Austin Warren, <u>Theory of Literature</u> (New York, 1949), pp. 106-7.

(book by two authors; pp. is the abbreviation of *pages*)

³ William Hickling Prescott, <u>History</u> <u>of</u> <u>the</u> <u>Reign</u>
<u>of</u> <u>Philip</u> <u>the</u> <u>Second,</u> <u>King</u> <u>of</u> <u>Spain,</u> ed. John Foster
Kirk (Philadelphia, 1871), II, 47.

(an edited work of more than one volume; *ed.* is the abbreviation
for "edited by"; note that whenever a volume number is cited, the
abbreviation p. or pp. is *not* used in front of the page number)

⁴ John Pick, ed., <u>The</u> <u>Windhover</u> (Columbus, Ohio
1968), p. 4.

(form for quotation from an editor's Introduction—as, for instance,
in this casebook series; here *ed.* is the abbreviation for "editor")

⁵ A.S.P. Woodhouse, "Nature and Grace in <u>The</u> <u>Faerie</u>
<u>Queen,</u>" in <u>Elizabethan</u> <u>Poetry</u>: <u>Modern</u> <u>Essays</u> <u>in</u>
<u>Criticism</u>, ed. Paul J. Alpers (New York, 1967),
pp. 346-7.

                    (chapter or article from an edited collection)

⁶ Morton D. Paley, "Tyger of Wrath," <u>PMLA</u>, LXXXI
(December, 1966), 544.

(an article from a periodical; note that because the volume number
is cited no p. or pp. precedes the page number; the titles of periodicals are often abbreviated in footnotes but are spelled out in the
Bibliography; here, for instance, *PMLA* is the abbreviation for
Publications of the Modern Language Association)

Secondary Footnotes

(Abbreviated footnote forms to be used after a work has been cited
once in full)

⁷ Baum, p. 45.

(abbreviated form for work cited in footnote #1; note that the
secondary footnote is indented the same number of spaces as the
first line of primary footnotes)

⁸ Wellek and Warren, pp. 239-40.

            (abbreviated form for work cited in footnote #2)

⁹ Prescott, II, 239.

(abbreviated form for work cited in footnote #3; because this is
a multi-volume work, the volume number must be given in addition to the page number)

¹⁰ <u>Ibid</u>., p. 245.

(refers to the immediately preceding footnote—that is, to page
245 in the second volume of Prescott's history; *ibid.* is the abbre-

viation of the Latin adverb *ibidem* meaning "in the same place"; note that this abbreviation is italicized or underlined and that it is followed by a period, because it is an abbreviation)

[11] Ibid., III, 103.

(refers to the immediately preceding footnote—that is, to Prescott's work again; there must be added to *ibid.* only what changes from the preceding footnote; here the volume and page changed; note that there is no p. before 103, because a volume number was cited)

[12] Baum, pp. 47-50.

(refers to the same work cited in footnote #7 and ultimately to the work cited in full in footnote #1)

[13] Paley, p. 547.

       (refers to the article cited in footnote #6)

[14] Rebecca P. Parkin, "Mythopoeic Activity in the Rape of the Lock," ELH, XXI (March, 1954), 32.

(since this article from the *Journal of English Literary History* has not been previously cited in full, it must be given in full here)

[15] Ibid., pp. 33-4.

(refers to Parkin's article in the immediately preceding footnote)

Bibliography Forms

Note carefully the differences in bibliography forms from footnote forms: (1) the last name of the author is given first, since bibliography items are arranged alphabetically according to the surname of the author (in the case of two or more authors of a work, only the name of the first author is reversed) ; (2) the first line of each bibliography item starts at the lefthand margin; subsequent lines are indented; (3) periods are used instead of commas, and parentheses do not enclose publication information; (4) the publisher is given in addition to the place of publication; (5) the first and last pages of articles and chapters are given; (6) most of the abbreviations used in footnotes are avoided in the Bibliography.

The items are arranged here alphabetically as they would appear in the Bibliography of your paper.

Baum, Paull F. Ten Studies in the Poetry of Matthew Arnold. Durham, N.C.: University of North Carolina Press, 1958.

Paley, Morton D. "Tyger of Wrath," Publications of
    the Modern Language Association, LXXXI (Decem-
    ber, 1966), 540-51.

Parkin, Rebecca P. "Mythopoeic Activity in the Rape
    of the Lock," Journal of English Literary
    History, XXI (March, 1954), 30-8.

Pick, John, editor. The Windhover. Columbus, Ohio:
    Charles E. Merrill Publishing Company, 1968.

Prescott, William Hickling. History of the Reign of
    Philip the Second, King of Spain. Edited by
    John Foster Kirk. 3 volumes. Philadelphia: J.B.
    Lippincott and Company, 1871.

Wellek, René and Austin Warren. Theory of Litera-
    ture. New York: Harcourt, Brace & World, Inc.,
    1949.

Woodhouse, A.S.P. "Nature and Grace in The Faerie
    Queene," in Elizabethan Poetry: Modern Essays in
    Criticism. Edited by Paul J. Alpers. New York:
    Oxford University Press, 1967, pp. 345-79.

If the form for some work that you are using in your paper is not given in these samples of footnote and bibliography entries, ask your instructor for advice as to the proper form.